Remembering Who We Are:
A Workbook

A Practical Guide to a Restored Life—
Based on an Adaptation of A.A.'s 12 Steps

For those recovering—
For those who desire spiritual growth

by

Carol Ann Preston

Bloomington, IN   Milton Keynes, UK
authorHOUSE

The examples given in this workbook are fictitious in nature and any resemblance to persons in real life is coincidental. These examples are intended to support and assist users of the workbook. In no instance is this workbook intended to take the place of professional guidance and counseling for those who are in need of it.

AuthorHouse™
1663 Liberty Drive, Suite 200
Bloomington, IN 47403
www.authorhouse.com
Phone: 1-800-839-8640

AuthorHouse™ UK Ltd.
500 Avebury Boulevard
Central Milton Keynes, MK9 2BE
www.authorhouse.co.uk
Phone: 08001974150

First published by AuthorHouse 02/06/06

ISBN: 1-4184-6232-2 (e)
ISBN: 1-4184-4692-0 (sc)

Library of Congress Control Number: 2004092138

Printed in the United States of America
Bloomington, Indiana

This book is printed on acid-free paper.

Cover design by Carol Ann Preston and John Randall Rouse
Editing and typesetting by Jeff Putnam, avenuepublishers@sbcglobal.net
Copyediting by Melissa Sharer

Scripture Quotations marked (NIV) are taken from the HOLY BIBLE, NEW INTERNATIONAL VERSION®, NIV®, COPYRIGHT© 1973, 1978, 1984 by International Bible Society. Used by permission. All rights reserved.

Disclaimer: The Twelve Steps are reprinted and adapted with permission of Alcoholics Anonymous World Services, Inc. (A.AW.S.) Permission to reprint and adapt the Twelve Steps does not mean that A.A.W.S. has reviewed or approved the contents of this publication, or that A.A.W.S. necessarily agrees with the views expressed herein. A.A. is a program of recovery from alcoholism *only*; use of the Twelve Steps in connection with programs and activities which are patterned after A.A., but which address other problems, or in any other non-A.A. context, does not imply endorsement of such programs or activities by any A.A. organization.

Foreword

PERHAPS THE MOST FAMOUS program in the world for recovery from addictions is the twelve-step program developed by the founders of Alcoholics Anonymous. This program, begun in the 1930's by Bill W. and Doctor Bob in the United States, has been used all over the world to deal with addiction not only to alcohol but to many other things—drugs, food, work, sex, etc.

Essential to the program is the recognition of dependence on a "Higher Power" (most of us would say "God") for help in the recovery process. Considerable influence in this area seems to have come from Father Ed Dowling, S.J., the spiritual director of Bill W.

In this workbook Carol Preston has developed a technique of working through each of the twelve steps, either as an individual or preferably in a relatively small group. Carol is imaginative and remarkably creative in these presentations, while at the same time never losing sight of the importance of the spiritual dimension. *Human help is important for recovery; God's help is essential.* The main point comes down to—"Get on your knees and beg God for help." This book is an excellent entrance into the whole process of recovery.

> Walter C. McCauley, S.J.
> Associate Director
> Montserrat Jesuit Retreat House
> Lake Dallas, Texas

For My husband, Ray

For walking this road of Faith with me—

As we both learn to receive God's Grace and Love,
As we learn to worship Him only,
As we are called to love our Creator,
each other, our neighbor,
and ourselves;
As we live, one day at a time, free.

Dedication

To God, my Higher Power, the loving and powerful Creator I acknowledge and thank for sending many guides into my life who supported not only the healing I needed, but the wholeness that I wanted. I dedicate this book to the Master Healer, my Savior Jesus Christ. He loves my soul no matter what and He guides my daily journey as my trusted friend. I thank Him for revealing His love to the deepest place within my own heart. I am truly blessed with love, strength and grace from the generous Heart of Jesus. I am grateful for the grace that allows for my human efforts to be a channel for God's love.

This book is also dedicated to my mother whom I thank so much for praying for me over the years, as she struggled to 'let go and let God' with each of her children, and for the unconditional love given as I was being restored to the daughter she knew me to be. I thank her, too, for the wisdom and acceptance she provides as she continues to become her most authentic self and my trusted friend. Trust and respect is truly the treasure we both share.

I also dedicate this book to Ray, my soul mate, my friend and my husband, whom I appreciate for believing in me when I could not and for his willingness to not give up when it would have been an easier, softer way. And to my children, Kari and Randy, I pray that your light will shine within this world and it will be a better place as you each add beauty, laughter and wonder while living, loving and serving. May you both find your way with safety, faith, love, and principles of integrity. May your life be one of honor, respect and trust.

I dedicate this workbook to all those who have been affected by alcoholism and other addictions as well as those who suffer from or with mental illness; to the mother, father, brother, sister, child or friend who suffer and feel unable to help the ones they love. I pray that someone will reach out to you with compassion and love, offering guidance for you and your loved ones, so that you will find the healing you long for and deserve.

My prayer for those who make use of this workbook is for your life to be the blessing it was created to be. I pray that you may find the joy of living and loving along with the joy of serving, for it is in serving that happiness truly lies and God's presence is experienced. May God's love flourish within you and your life.

May we each pause, one day at a time, to recognize the loving presence of God reflected in our daily life and also within each other.

My hope is that God will bring hope to those situations filled with hopelessness, and that Divine love, courage and honesty will find its way into the minds and hearts of hopeless alcoholics or addicts, and others who are suffering from the ill effects of alcoholism and other addictions.

Acknowledgments

MY THANKS TO THE MANY WOMEN AND MEN who were willing to trust the process set forth in this workbook and to commit their time, resources, and work to use the tools outlined in this book as an instrument for personal restoration. Thanks also to those who offered their experience, ideas and suggestions as this workbook evolved over the past several years.

I appreciate not only the many women who shared their experience with me over the course of 20 years in the practical use of the 12 steps and principles from A.A., but also one particular man, who has requested personal and professional anonymity. Through his work with Native American alcoholics in a prison setting, and by means of the methods he used to minister and teach them, I learned to apply mind-mapping within the framework of A.A.'s 12 steps. By observing his work and heeding his guidance I was able to understand how my perceptions or misperceptions were fueling my resentments.

Finally I was able to understand how the problem really did center within my mind. This awareness had eluded me for years, but armed with willingness and honesty I was able to see that my problems in living truly derived from the many misperceptions that had bound me to resentments. This understanding released me from bondage and became the path that led to my desired freedom.

I can not thank Melissa Sharer enough, as it was she who committed many hours of her time and talent to assist me in countless ways with the creation of this workbook. Her friendship is a treasure and our time together laughing and crying as we walked through our own healing is precious to me. Thanks also to Jeff Putnam for editing this workbook. I appreciate his honesty and humor, as this is always delivered with kindness. I cannot adequately express my thanks to Jeff for his commitment to the workbook and for encouraging my efforts as a writer. Thanks also to my dear and trusted friend, Kathleen for her suggestions. Thanks most of all for her gentle guidance, wisdom and honesty, as well as her commitment to minister to others and her commitment to daily prayer. She is my spiritual teacher.

Thanks to June for being the friend of Bill W.'s that you have been for over 25 years. By sharing your wisdom and laughter, and by showing me what trust could be, you made a difference in my life and countless others. Thanks to Gayle for teaching me the in-depth application of many of the tools outlined within this workbook. Your experience and guidance led me to a more intimate relationship with God and an appreciation of Creation.

I also appreciate my dear friend Lisa Walsh for being a living example of what unselfish love *looks like*. To Dr. Patricia Suppes, a leading physician in the mental health field, I appreciate your efforts in bringing to light the inaccurate diagnosis and treatment of the bipolar illness that I lived with for twelve years, and in setting the record straight. Thank you for your professional efforts toward the teaching of more accurate and effective methods in the diagnosis of bipolar illness and effective treatment for those who suffer with it.

Thanks to Alcoholics Anonymous for allowing me to adapt the steps for this workbook and for the brief quotes from *Alcoholics Anonymous*.

Thanks also to the International Bible Society for graciously allowing me to reprint quotes from the New International Version Bible. Your readiness to grant these permissions has been greatly appreciated.

Twelve Steps of Alcoholics Anonymous

STEP ONE
"We admitted we were powerless over alcohol."

STEP TWO
"Came to believe that a Power greater than ourselves could restore us to sanity."

STEP THREE
"Made a decision to turn our will and our lives over to the care of God, as we understood Him."

STEP FOUR
"Made a searching and fearless moral inventory of ourselves."

STEP FIVE
"Admitted to God, to ourselves, and to another human being the exact nature of our wrongs."

STEP SIX
"Were entirely ready to have God remove all these defects of character."

STEP SEVEN
"Humbly asked Him to remove our shortcomings."

STEP EIGHT
"Made a list of all persons we had harmed, and became willing to make amends to them all."

STEP NINE
"Made direct amends to such people wherever possible, except when to do so would injure them or others."

STEP TEN
"Continued to take personal inventory and when we were wrong promptly admitted it."

STEP ELEVEN
"Sought through prayer and meditation to improve our conscious contact with God, as we understood Him, praying only for knowledge of His will for us and the power to carry that out."

STEP TWELVE
"Having had a spiritual awakening as the result of these steps, we tried to carry this message to alcoholics, and to practice these principles in all our affairs."

CONTENTS

Twelve Step Group Directory

This is a partial list of Twelve Step Groups; additional groups may be located in your local telephone or city directory

Alcoholics Anonymous—Support for those who have a desire to stop drinking. For information, write to: Alcoholics Anonymous World Services, Inc., Grand Central Station, PO Box 459, New York, NY 10163 or call (212) 870-3400 or check your local phone book.
http://www.alcoholics-anonymous.org/

Al-Anon—Support & Recovery for family or friend of alcoholics. For information, write to: Al-Anon Family Group Headquarters, Inc., 1600 Corporate Landing Parkway, Virginia Beach, VA 23454-5617 or call (888) 425-2666 or check your local phone book.
http://www.al-anon.org/

Alateen is part of the Alanon Family program and is typically for teens whose lives have been affected by another person's drinking. For information, call (888) 425-2666 or check your local phone book for Alanon Family group for meeting information.
http://www.al-anon.alateen.org/index.html

Emotions Anonymous—Support & Recovery for those suffering from a variety of emotional difficulties. For information, write to: Emotions Anonymous International, PO Box 4245, St. Paul, MN 55104-0245 or call (651) 647-9712.
http://www.emotionsanonymous.org/

Families Anonymous—Support & Recovery for family or friends of those with alcohol, drug or behavioral problems. For information, write to: Families Anonymous, Inc. PO Box 3475, Culver City, CA 90231 or call (800) 736-9805.
http://www.familiesanonymous.org/

Narcotics Anonymous—Support & Recovery for all drug addicts. For information, write to: Narcotics Anonymous, World Service Office, PO Box 9999, Van Nuys, CA 91409 or call (818) 773-9999 or check your local phone book. For information, outside of the US, write to: WSO Europe, 48 Rue de l'Ete/Zomerstraat, B-1050 Brussels, Belgium or call 32-2-646-6012.
http://www.na.org/index.htm

Nar-Anon Family Groups—Support & Recovery program for family and friends of drug abusers. For information, write to: Nar-Anon Family Group Headquarters, Inc., PO Box 2562, Palos Verdes Peninsula, CA 90274 or call (310) 547-5800.
http://www.naranoncalifornia.org/

Nicotine Anonymous—Support & Recovery for those who would like to stop using tobacco and nicotine products in any form. For information, write to: Nicotine Anonymous World Services, 419 Main Street, PMB# 370, Huntington Beach, CA 92648 or
call (415) 750-0328.
http://www.nicotine-anonymous.org/

Overeaters Anonymous—Support & Recovery from compulsive overeating. For information, write to: World Service Office, PO Box 44020, Rio Rancho, NM 87174-4020 or call (505) 891-2664.
http://www.oa.org/

Compulsive Eaters Anonymous—HOW—Support & Recovery for compulsive eating and food addiction with a disciplined and structured approach using the 12 Steps & 12 Traditions. For information, write to: Compulsive Eaters Anonymous-HOW, 5500 East Atherton Street, Suite 227-B, Long Beach, CA 90815-4017 or
call (562) 342-9344.
http://www.ceahow.org/

Sex and Love Addicts Anonymous (SLAA)—Support & Recovery to counter the addictive behaviors related to sex and love addiction and its dependencies. For information, write to: Fellowship Wide Services, PO Box 338, Norwood, MA 02062-0338 or call (781) 255-8825.
http://www.slaafws.org/index.html

Sex Addicts Anonymous (SAA)—Support & Recovery from sexual addiction. For information, write to: ISO of SAA, PO Box 70949, Houston, TX 77270 or call (713) 869-4902 or (800) 477-8191.
http://www.sexaa.org/

Debtors Anonymous—Support & Recovery for those whose lives are unmanageable due to credit card debt or overspending. For information, write to: Debtors Anonymous General Service Office, PO Box 920888, Needham, MA 02492-0009 or
call (781) 453-2743.
http://www.debtorsanonymous.org/

Gamblers Anonymous—Support & Recovery for those with a desire to stop gambling. For information, write to: Gamblers Anonymous International Service Office, PO Box 17173, Los Angeles, CA 90017 or call (213) 386-8789.
http://www.gamblersanonymous.org/

Resources and Help

Childhelp USA National Child Abuse hotline (24 hours)
Confidential toll free assistance for any child being abused and wanting help,
frustrated parents seeking help, or for adults or children needing a local phone
number to report child abuse.
1-800-4-A-CHILD

CDC National AIDS Hotline (24 hours)
1-800-342-2437

Cocaine hotline (24 hours)
1-800-262-2463 or 1-800-COCAINE

Suicide Hotline
1-800-784-2433

The Trevor Helpline—Suicide prevention for the questioning or gay youth
1-800-850-8078

National Foundation for Depressive Illness, Inc.
1-800-248-4344

Rape, Abuse, & Incest National Network (RAINN) operates the
National Sexual Assault Hotline
1-800-656-HOPE

National Runaway Switchboard & National Adolescent Suicide Hotline
1-800-621-4000

Your Church, mental health provider, city directory or telephone book may
provide additional support information.

Remembering Who We Are:
A Workbook

**A Practical Guide to a Restored Life—
Based on an Adaptation of A.A.'s 12 Steps**

*For those recovering—
For those who desire spiritual growth*

Introduction

I FIRST HEARD about twelve step anonymous groups in 1979 from a parish priest. I was discussing the difficulty I was having with some of my family relationships and he suggested I try the twelve step approach in solving my problems. During this same time I was seriously attempting once again to develop a personal relationship with God—one that was more than going to Sunday church service and confessing my sins. I must admit I had not practiced complete honesty during my confessionals, since I was too embarrassed to tell the "whole" truth. In any case, when this priest suggested I attend a twelve step group I could see no point in doing so, as I was convinced the problem was simple. It was them, not me! If "they" would change, my life would be fine. I later learned how very wrong I was. I ignored his recommendation and went about my life managing it the best I could. Like most over-achievers I resolved to try harder and do more. Only as a last resort, when all else failed, would I seek to escape the pain of living—the pain of loving. Anything that would ease the pain was okay: worry, boredom, obsessing on others, perfectionism, alcohol, 'fixing' others, anger, work, staying busy, etc. It would be a few more years before I was capable of enough honesty about myself to see that I was the one in need of help—and a few more years still before Grace would call my name and allow me to see that *the problem in my life was me,* so that I could finally see a solution! What I found was a simple path that led me to a belief in and an intimate relationship with God—a God Who could solve all of my problems.

The One Who was strong enough to solve my problems, a God I could rely upon, was not a projection of my emotions. I needed simple direction to find Him and find a relationship with Him in which every area of my life would matter. I came to see that it was in my nature to have this spiritual need met. Yet I had no idea that I would develop this type of relationship with a God of my understanding through the process of using the twelve steps from *Alcoholics Anonymous.* I had attended church faithfully; taught religious education and prayed daily (pleading, mostly) and I had no idea what grace or spiritual discipline meant. I had tried to earn God's help and love and had failed miserably. When all my efforts failed I would seek escape. Only when all these escapes failed was I willing enough—honest enough—to see that Grace is a gift, not to be earned but received.

After applying the twelve steps and principles to my life several times over a period of years I discussed my relationship with God and my place in this life with a trusted priest, who has since heard a number of my Fifth Steps. I felt then as though I were walking in the desert—that my life had been laid to waste mentally, spiritually and emotionally. I had a husband, children, was active again in my church, going to college, doing volunteer work, but a void within me was still unfilled. I had been afraid—afraid that if I "let go," when it came right down to it I would not matter, at least not as much to anyone else as I did to myself. This had always been my biggest conflict—being human and spiritual at the same time. This was the source of my misery and aloneness. How was I to achieve my potential as both a human and a spiritual being? How was I to achieve the spiritual and personal maturity I desired, not controlled by dogma and rules, but guided by love in my development?

I had longed for this even as a young teen, and experienced much conflict. I had only found answers that would drown or quiet the spiritual voice that called my name—or I would go to the other extreme. Neither way worked, so happiness that was born from within was elusive. The process I will reveal in this workbook served to integrate both of these aspects of my nature, and has done so over and over again. It has taken time, but it has happened. No longer would I try to destroy the God in me, the good in me under the false belief that I must be perfect to find a life of happy usefulness.

I had come to believe in my own mind that I had no value to God as a woman, a woman who desired to be a wife and mother and to serve the Creator, the Divine Spirit. I tried to drown the pain of this idea. This was the biggest "old idea" of them all—and it had to go. Finally it did. I have a place, as we all do. There is a place for all who seek to serve.

Years after meeting this priest I reached out to a friend, Gayle, to assist me in healing a troubled relationship. I had been practicing spiritual principles for many years by this time, when there was a crisis in another of my relationships. As it turned out I was to experience healing and restoration beyond my wildest dreams.

Gayle had been shown how to apply mind mapping, affirmations and visioning to the twelve steps and she helped me to do the same. Gayle guided me in the use of letter writing in making direct amends, to those I had hurt. There is written guidance in the Bible (Matthew 5:23-24) as to how our relationships with others may be amended so that love, forgiveness, mercy and peace can become the foundation of our lives. The passage where Jesus tells his followers to go and reconcile with their brothers before offering a gift at the altar of God has stayed with me. By making direct amends in this way I found peace.

Through guidance and support I was able to be honest in examining the nature of my wrongs, which originated in my perception, my thinking. I had by now received—as well—support to discover my hopes, dreams and desires, which also had been hidden. It took as much courage to bring to light my true heart's desire as it did to look at my faults.

Over the years that I was growing as a spiritual woman I learned that those who will support me in being all of who I am and all that God created me to be are those who are willing to grow themselves. Maybe they are growing in a different way, but the support to look at glaring defects of character, and the support to give up that which is harmful—well, that kind of support is hard to come by. Most of us want to be liked by our peers. I have found that letting go of my old ideas of who I was and uncovering who I was created to be has been at best an awkward and difficult process. And it has taken a long time. For some it does not take so much work or effort, but others will embark on the healing process with many wounds to heal. It was that way for me; it took many years before I was able to see myself as the loving, talented and kind person God created me to be. When I got past the pain of growing up, the joy of living and loving had the same depth as my pain had formerly. I was blessed in equal measure. I found that I am a woman of courage and I have been blessed as a result of that courage. I had come face to face with my powerlessness over alcohol (regardless of who drinks it), death, money, abuse, jobs, the Catholic Church, relationships, etc. And through the recovery process I have found as much freedom and restoration as I was willing to hope and dream for. I found God deep within—the last place I wanted to look.

This courage is open to all, as courage is nothing more than fear taking action based upon faith—a gift of grace found through honesty.

In a book called *The Soul of Sponsorship*, one of the cofounders of Alcoholics Anonymous, Bill W., communicated in a letter written to his spiritual director, Father Ed Dowling, that he could see the need for an in-depth working of the twelve steps. This workbook is a tool that supports this idea. Having used this process a number of times, referring each time in greater detail to the wording in the book *Alcoholics Anonymous*, I began to have an awakening to the God of my understanding and the wonder of life. I truly have been reborn (as the book promises) and restored to the woman I was created to be. I have since enjoyed a quality of life I wouldn't have thought possible, though in my heart I had always hoped for my personal transformation. It just took a while.

Creating this guide, with full knowledge that there have been a number of "step guides" making the rounds, I brought together tools that I found to be the most effective. In each case I made sure the tools were in support of the steps as set forth in *Alcoholics Anonymous*, and applicable to those of diverse religious affiliations and backgrounds, or none at all. Many experiences have shown that one does not have to be dying to muster the kind of courage and honesty it takes to complete this process. In fact anyone who desires a life filled with purpose and healing may benefit from this guide.

Though at first glance it may seem simple, it is sometimes hard to walk this path. The path was laid out years ago, first in the Bible and later in more simple language by a couple of drunks trying to share their methods for recovery from a seemingly hopeless disease. Still, you cannot go wrong with this guide as long as you are making a sincere effort, and you are honest. I promise that if you complete this guide your life will be different and more in line with the dreams held within your heart. I believe that the biggest conflict most of us have arises from a lack of harmony between our human and our divine nature. This guide will help to uncover things that have prevented that harmony and it will help you develop a relationship with God that can solve your problems, restore your life and help you to remember who you are—a perfect creation of God.

A miracle of healing and restoration has been prepared especially for you. Do not desire the healing of another, or miracles of another—look for yours. You will discover God's blessings and live in an intimate relationship with Him simply by being your most authentic self.

Mind Mapping

Mind Mapping was produced and promoted by Tony Buzan as an educational tool. For a complete explanation of this technique, see *The Mind Map* by Tony Buzan.

Visioning

Visioning (or creating "affirmation statements") has been used for years in many fields. Sales and motivational training teach that you need to know not only where you are, but also where you are going. A good business always has a vision or mission statement. Professional mental health experts use affirmations as a support tool for clients.

All that is needed during this process is this workbook, pen and paper, trustworthy support and the book, *Alcoholics Anonymous*, for reference. This process could take six to nine months, and may be experienced individually or in a group. Suggested guidelines for group studies can be found in the last chapter. Make sure to read your work for each step to your designated support person (not a family member).

Having support during this process is crucial. You deserve support, so look around and find someone committed to seeing you through this. You may work the steps using this process time and time again. As you experience restoration the mapping and visioning and even the inventory get easier.

Before you begin this process reflect on the words below and imagine the truth as it pertains to your life today. Ask yourself one simple question—are you willing to remember who you are?

Gone are the days when my life was guided by emotions, gone are the days when my heart and my mind are living in the past, fearing mistakes to be made in the future. Gone are the days lived with unrealistic expectations leaving all with disappointment.

Today my life is not measured by what you think of me, what you do for me, or I what I do for you. Today my life is measured by love, love that has been freely given to me. Freely this Divine love protected me, guided me, healed parts of me beyond what I would have thought possible. With Grace, Divine love has transformed me to become the creation I was intended to be, with purpose and beauty, free to love others.

Today my life is measured and guided by principle, not perfection or personality; today I am free to live, to love, to let go.

Carol Preston

Old Ideas

One of the interesting things in the book, *Alcoholics Anonymous*, is a statement implying that one must let go of all of one's old ideas to be able to recover and heal. I have found that letting go of old ideas is hard at best. It does not say which old ideas; the good or the bad. It simply states that one must let go of all of them. To let go is to create room for current and possibly more accurate ideas that may work better for you. Some examples of "old ideas" are below.

Sample Old Ideas

I am not worthy

I am not lovable

I am stupid

I am unique and so are my problems

Women are victims

Men are victims

Doctors are always right

Clergy/Ministers are perfect and always right

I must be perfect, mistakes are not allowed

I am not a good employee if I take time off

Keep secrets – Don't tell

Men/Women are always right

Children are to be seen and not heard

Don't question anyone, i.e. authority figures

I am only wanted as a provider / for money

I am only wanted for sex

I am not wanted

Happiness only comes in the "hereafter"

There is no life after death

If I am good or perfect no one will leave me

I am basically a bad person, no one wants me

I am defective

It is up to me to keep the family together

It is up to me to get things done

There is never enough

Money buys happiness

I'm just unlucky

I am going to hell

I can never be forgiven

God made a mistake with me / I am a mistake

My life is a mistake

I must be right at all times

Don't ever show your fear, anger, pain

I'm too old to change

I'm too young to know anything

No one really understands

Trust no one

Addicts are bad people

It is my fault if my children become addicts or make terrible mistakes

I will go to hell for questioning or doubting religious authority

---

Add a few "old ideas" of your own that you would be *willing* to let go of.

1.

2.

3.

4.

You get the idea. Keep an open mind and heart and you will experience the healing you have longed for. Be *willing* to let go of your old ideas, and then you may decide at a later time to select the ideas of your past that are worth retaining. This is a time to unlearn ideas that you are not certain are yours to begin with.

"I know that nothing good lives in me, that is, in my sinful nature. For I have the desire to do what is good, but I cannot carry it out."
Romans 7: 18 (NIV)

Chapter One
Support for Step One

I CAN PROMISE you one thing at this point. If you are willing to be completely honest and put onto paper what your life is like for you today—in it's powerlessness and unmanageability—then you are on the road to freedom.

I have found that each time I use this tool and process it gets easier and easier. The struggle is easier and the fear is less with each step. The First Step states "we are powerless over alcohol..." it does not state "we are powerless over the alcoholic." I have faced my powerlessness over alcohol, drugs, food, death and money. Has it been painful to do the writing? Of course! Writing how my powerlessness created unmanageability was even more painful. It was hard to look at the adverse affects, but at the same time, liberating finally to face the truth and know that I would be set free as I moved into Step Two.

In this process no one gets to tell you that your reality is wrong. This is a process to get out of your head and heart and put your reality on paper. The problem of the alcoholic, as explained in the book, *Alcoholics Anonymous,* centers in his/her mind. So find out what is in that mind of yours and put it on paper. No matter how ugly or silly it may seem, if it exists in your mind then it is real. My mind and heart was a painful place to go at one time. Therefore I avoided it at times, struggling to control that which I couldn't control, in particular those things I felt were "my fault." Faced with putting down on paper what was out of control in my life, *things I could not exert control over,* I found myself listing a number of things that I wanted to believe were my fault. I was under the delusion that, being responsible for the outcome of another's life, behavior, etc., meant that I would be powerful enough to correct and manage it. "I am powerless..." That is a tough place to go—hard to admit on paper, hard to share with another.

But here is the deal. If you don't know where you are, how are you going to know where you are going? You have to start by looking at where you are right now without judgement.

And for those who have a relationship with God, great! I have found that *unless I continue to enlarge my spiritual condition, my usefulness to God and others is bound to be limited at best.* I will fall prey to my own powerlessness again if I do not continue to grow. Making lists (mind mapping) is part of this growth process, a tool to support spiritual growth.

A note of strong encouragement if you find yourself with severe periods of depression that interfere with your ability to participate in your life, or if you lack feelings of pleasure and are unable to maintain your personal or professional interests for more than several weeks. If this is your experience then it is strongly suggested that you seek the assistance of a mental health professional or doctor as soon as possible. Ask family or friends if they can refer you to a good and helpful doctor, or ask appropriate human resources people where you work—or you can ask your family doctor for a reference to a reliable and understanding mental health professional.

Medical depression is readily treated today and no one needs to suffer unnecessarily. This is not about being a weak person; this is an illness that requires the care of a doctor. An estimated 35 to 40 million Americans will suffer from depression during some period in their lives. Too many times shame and old ideas about not being able to "pick yourself up by the boot straps" interfere and stand in the way of good medical help. We all feel "down" sometimes and we all feel grief as we experience losses, but if these feelings are prolonged and interfere with your ability to enjoy life, then be good to yourself and get a professional evaluation. This small action may also give you peace of mind as you go forward with the recovery process as it is addressed in this workbook.

Some final advice: a doctor you trust will be able to rule out medical conditions besides depression that may be at issue. And medical professionals can recognize and treat many types of depression or illnesses where depression plays a part, such as bipolar disorder, which features some mood swings from extreme lows to extreme highs. Medications to treat these illnesses can now be prescribed that do not create feelings of euphoria, and once they have taken effect, a previously depressed person can readily address problems relative to the illness. Seek help immediately if the aforementioned symptoms describe your current state, then continue with this workbook with the care and support of a mental health professional.

One Thing to Remember -
God is never Late.

How to Begin

Reading *Alcoholics Anonymous,* as a reference, through this process is essential - as you read - highlight the three "P's", Prayers, Promises and Principles.

Experience has shown that it's best to begin writing in a quiet space, with no possibility of interruption, working for about an hour at any given time. Please try it! I took a deep breath and put on paper how the "powerless" seemed to be for me, what it "looked like." I have been asked what I mean by, "What it looked like." Examples of mind mapping follow. This is not the place for explanations. Simply put down words that flow as you focus on the *one thing*. The words that flowed with the word (*one thing*) alcohol were: death, fear, pain, embarrassment, shame, hopeless, failure, etc. What are the words that portray your world, your life with "it"—alcohol or whatever it is that you have little or no control over? Remember it does not matter who is actually using the "it" to cause problems for you.

I also did Step One over food. Though I have not abused food, I have loved many people in my life who have. Areas of my life had become unmanageable as a result of my feeling responsible for controlling overeaters. Seeing those I love misuse food created fear for me that I would lose them to an early death and it would be my fault. (My life had thus become unmanageable.) One last example for powerlessness. If someone other than you rages, it causes problems and pain in your life. You cannot make another stop the raging; therefore you are powerless over rage. How does that play out in your life? What does your world look like with rage as something you cannot stop? How about, fear, pain, abuse, shame, broken promises, ended relationships, anger, hate, terror, death, etc. For some of you, the mind maps may look very similar regardless of what the powerlessness is about. If you are using this process and sharing with a group and each person is writing about a different *thing* for powerlessness, you may find that several people have similar mind maps. Often our lives uncovered look very much alike.

Use feeling words, adjectives or brief statements in your mind maps showing how each area looks/seems in your life. Some areas may look the same, and some areas will have more written about them than others. When complete, share your Step One mind maps with your support person or with your small group. Avoid explanation or analysis, simply read the words written on your Step One mind maps without interruption.

After sharing your Step One mind maps with your support person you may ask and receive encouragement, so that your willingness and honesty in this step can be acknowledged before moving on to Step Two.

Be specific. You can do this!

Chapter One
STEP ONE
Part One

*We have admitted we are powerless over _____, and
our lives have become unmanageable.*

Powerless—to be or experience being without sufficient strength

*What do you have little or no control over in your life today?
What is the primary thing that is causing unmanageability in your life?*

📖   **Read** from the preface of *Alcoholics Anonymous* to the chapter titled "We Agnostics." See how you relate to the powerlessness revealed in these pages. If alcohol is not your problem *today*, then replace the word alcohol with the *one thing* you are currently dealing with. *Pray* for acceptance over your lack of power and the unmanageability created in your life.

There may be more than *one thing* identified for what you are "powerless" over, but try to focus your attention to *one thing* that is primarily interfering with your happiness and joy, and relationship with God and with others.

Here is a suggested list to select from: alcohol, drugs, food, rage, sex, money (hoarding, illicit activity or compulsive spending), family, death, illness or health-related issues of yours or another's, work, your weight or another person's weight, nicotine, mental illness, divorce, abuse, gambling, religion, institutions, the IRS or government, church or medical community.

If any of these areas listed is a problem for a loved one and adversely affects you, then you can no longer say to yourself "It's not my problem." If you have been trying to exert control over your loved ones' problems, and your efforts have created unmanageability, list this *one thing* that you are powerless over, whether it be alcohol, food, drugs, work, gambling, etc.

*Remember that this mind map does not negate the things that are
manageable in your life, it merely helps you to examine an
area of powerlessness and its effect on your life today.*

✍   **Complete a mind map for the area of powerlessness in your life today.**

📖   **Read this mind map to your support person as soon as it is completed!**

PRINCIPLE

Honesty

Chapter One

STEP ONE MIND MAP
Part One
Example

Powerless Over   <u>Alcohol</u>

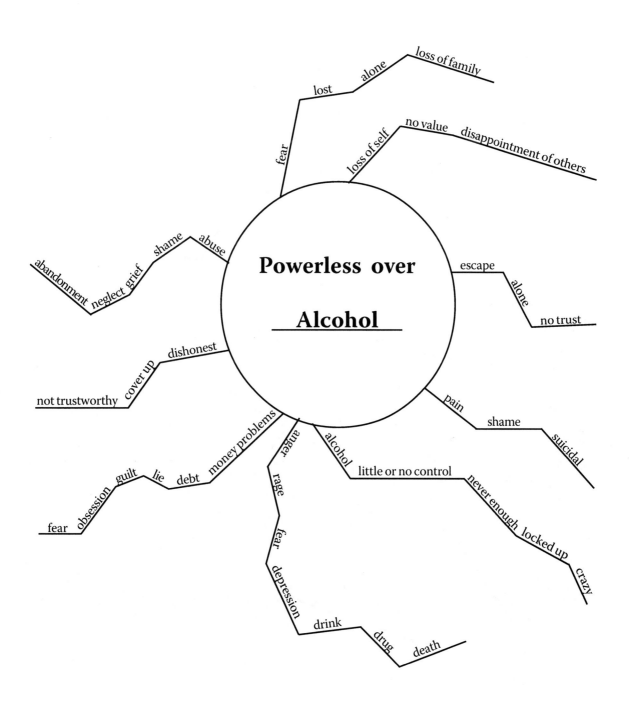

STEP ONE MIND MAP
Part One

Powerless Over _____

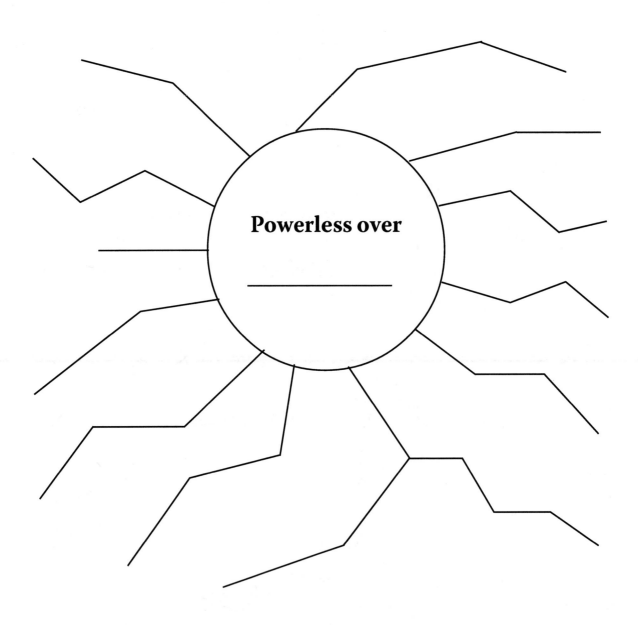

Chapter One
STEP ONE
Part Two

📖 ***Read*** page 52 of *Alcoholics Anonymous*; pay attention to the third paragraph as it points out nine areas of human problems. These are the areas addressed in this step and Step Two. Examine each of these nine areas of your life and describe how unmanageability presents itself in your life today as a result of the powerlessness you are addressing now.

✍ ***Complete a mind map for each of the nine problem areas listed below.***

I recommend completing no more than three mind maps at a time. This will allow your mind to rest and bring fresh reflection to each area. You may notice that some areas appear similar (and this is common), or you may find as you write your mind maps that some of the areas listed below are not as unmanageable as other areas—others have experienced the same thing. You can do no wrong as long as you are honest in your efforts. As you commit yourself to writing you will gain confidence with your efforts to make an honest appraisal of your life as it appears today.

Nine Areas of Human Problems:
1. Trouble with personal relationships
2. Difficulty controlling our emotional nature
3. Falling prey to misery
4. Falling prey to depression
5. Trouble making a living—include finances, money, your 'job' as a student, home-maker, company executive
6. Feelings of uselessness
7. Feeling full of fear
8. Being unhappy
9. Unable to be of real help to others

📖 ***Read each mind map to your support person as soon as it is completed.***

PRINCIPLE *Honesty*

STEP ONE MIND MAP
Part Two
Example

Area of Unmanageability
Personal Relationships

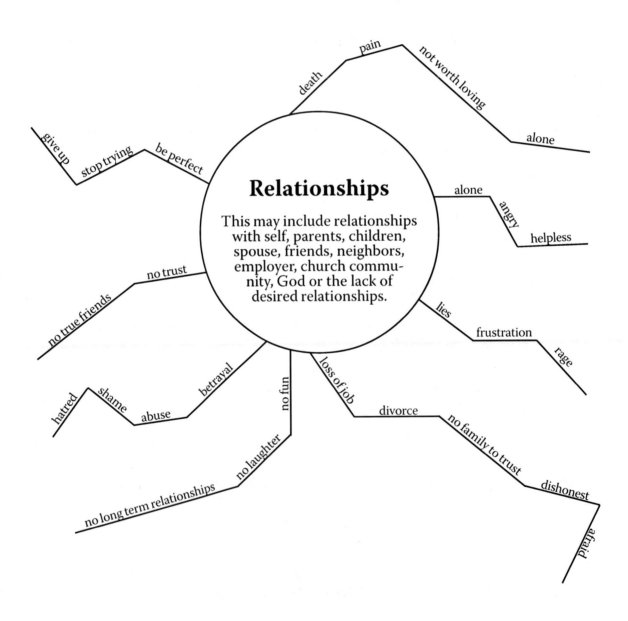

STEP ONE MIND MAP
Part Two
Example

Area of Unmanageability
Emotional Nature

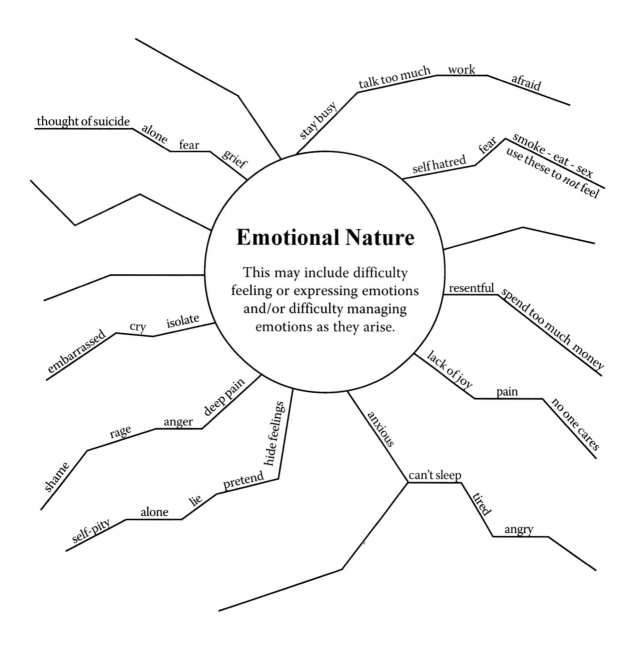

STEP ONE MIND MAP
Part Two
Example

Area of Unmanageability
Prey to Misery

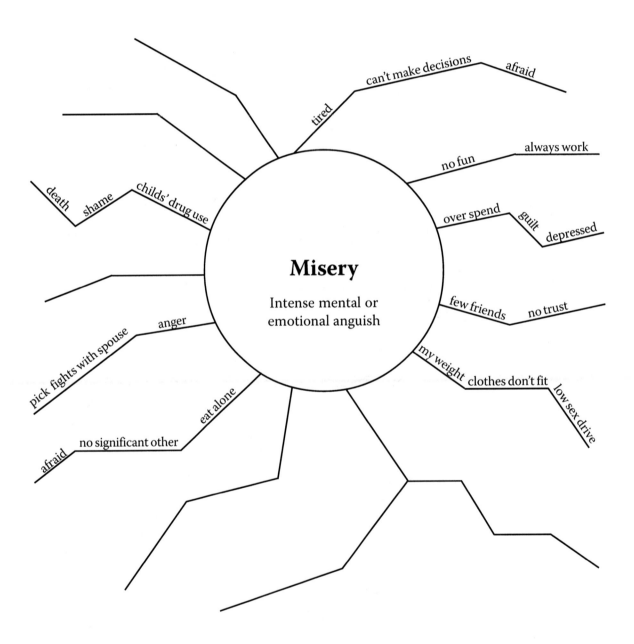

STEP ONE MIND MAP
Part Two
Example

Area of Unmanageability
Prey to Depression

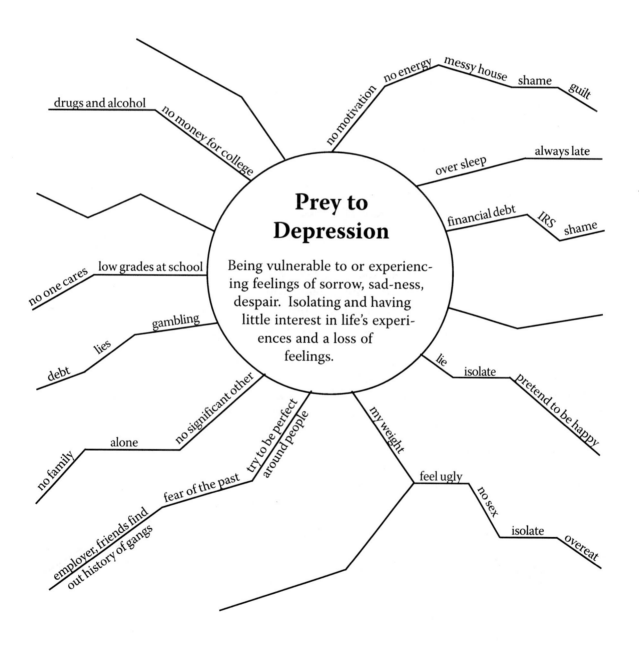

STEP ONE MIND MAP
Part Two
Example

Area of Unmanageability
Can't Make a Living

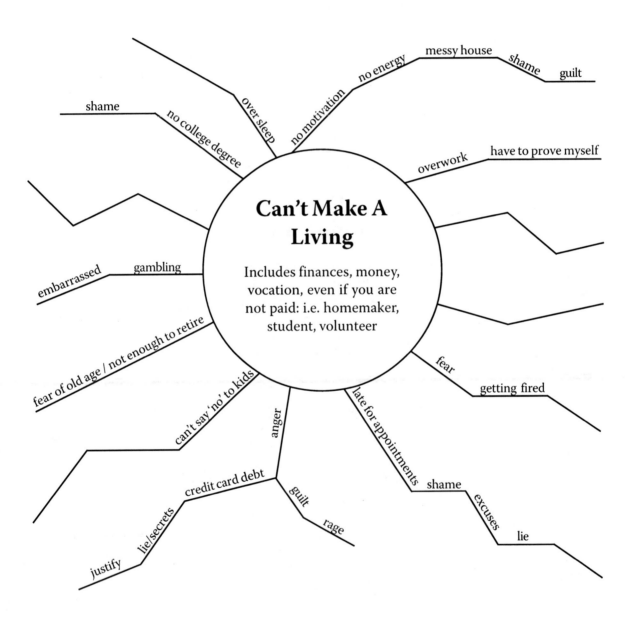

STEP ONE MIND MAP
Part Two
Example

Area of Unmanageability
Feeling of Uselessness

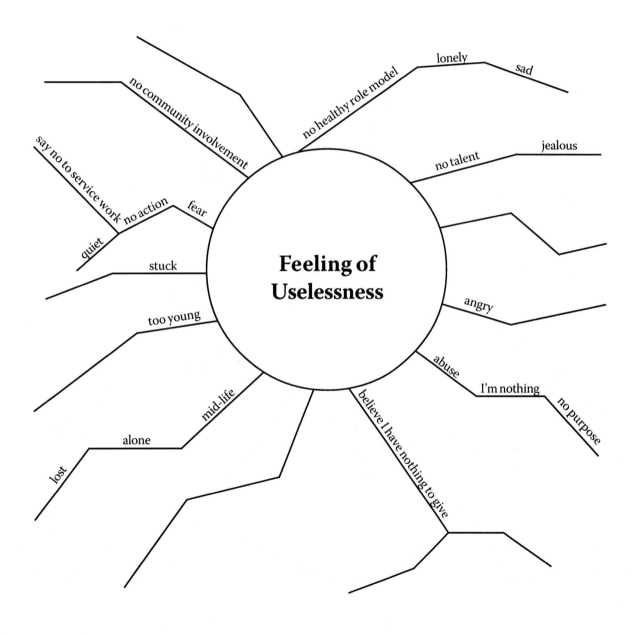

STEP ONE MIND MAP
Part Two
Example

Area of Unmanageability
Full of Fear

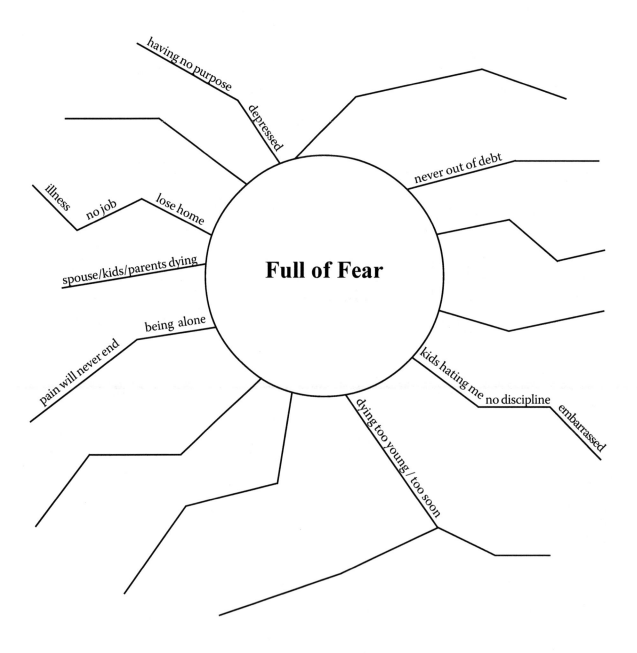

STEP ONE MIND MAP
Part Two
Example

Area of Unmanageability
We are Unhappy

feel ugly

no partner

no dad — missed out — sad — alone

don't feel wanted — blame others

no nice clothes — weight

isolate — bankrupt

We Are Unhappy

spouse / self / parents always at work

overwork

misuse money — never enough

alone

physical pain

can't sleep

no help / no relief — alone

tired — angry — late to work

STEP ONE MIND MAP
Part Two
Example

Area of Unmanageability
Can't be of Real Help to Others

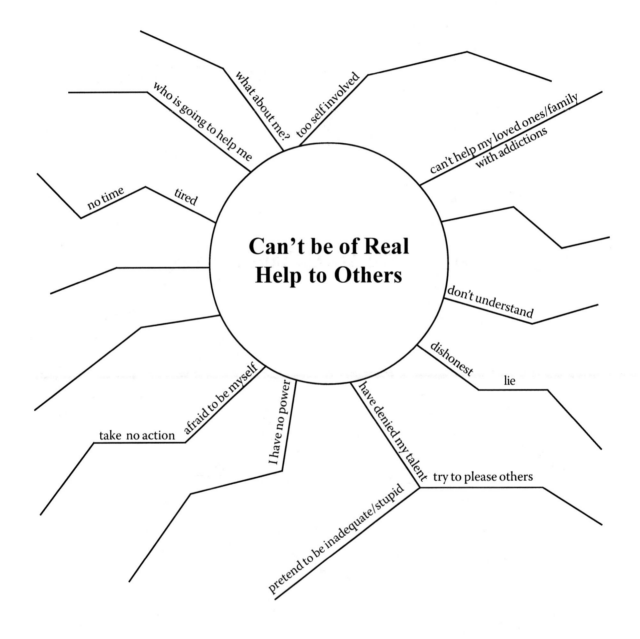

STEP ONE MIND MAP
Part Two

Area of Unmanageability
Personal Relationships

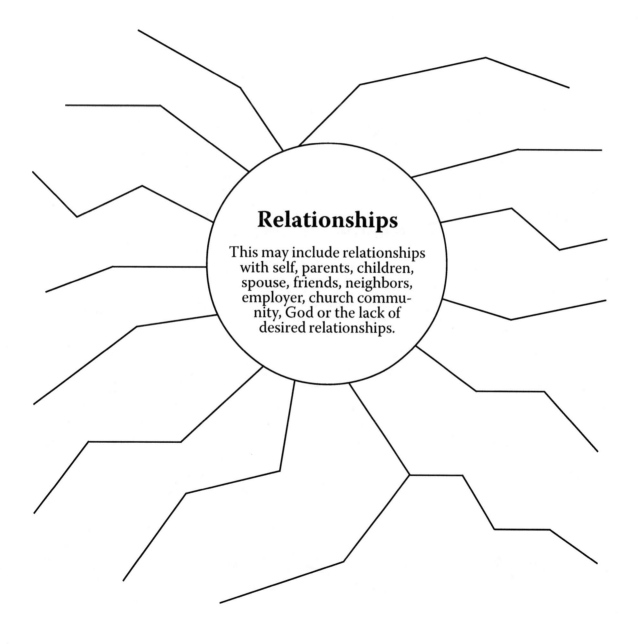

Relationships

This may include relationships with self, parents, children, spouse, friends, neighbors, employer, church community, God or the lack of desired relationships.

STEP ONE MIND MAP
Part Two

Area of Unmanageability
Emotional Nature

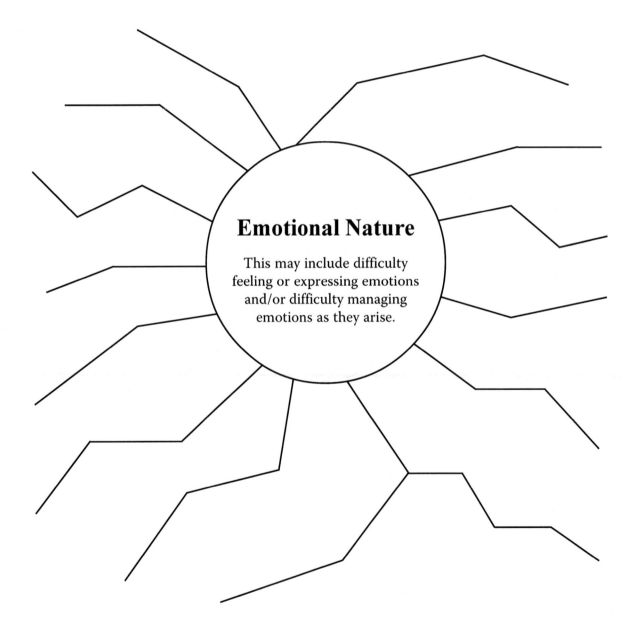

Emotional Nature

This may include difficulty feeling or expressing emotions and/or difficulty managing emotions as they arise.

STEP ONE MIND MAP
Part Two

Area of Unmanageability
Prey to Misery

Prey to Misery

Being vulnerable to or experiencing intense mental and/or emotional suffering or pain. How is misery reflected in your life?

STEP ONE MIND MAP
Part Two

Area of Unmanageability
Prey to Depression

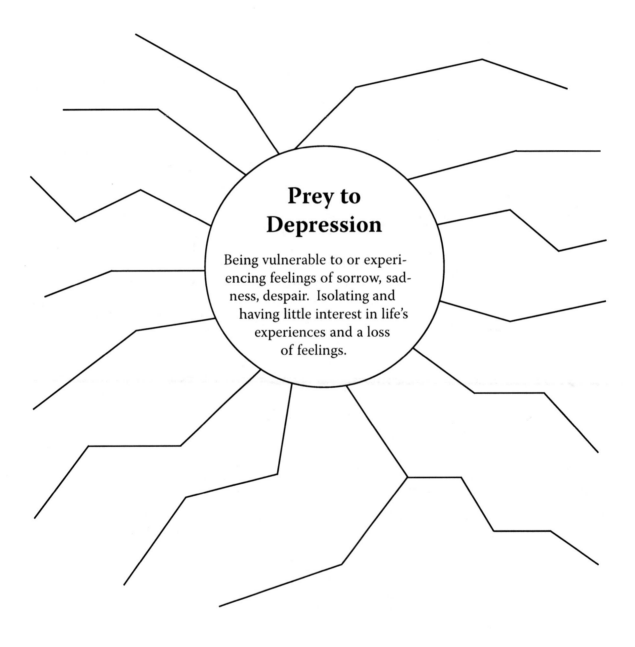

Prey to Depression

Being vulnerable to or experiencing feelings of sorrow, sadness, despair. Isolating and having little interest in life's experiences and a loss of feelings.

STEP ONE MIND MAP
Part Two

Area of Unmanageability
Can't Make a Living

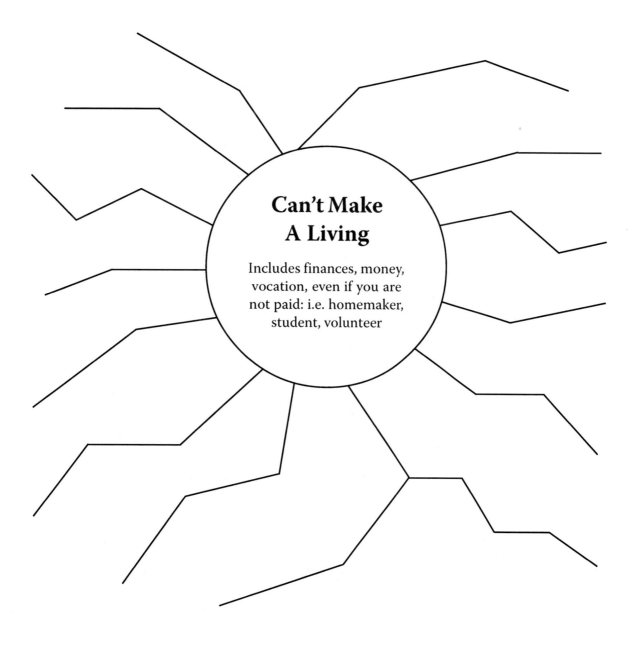

**Can't Make
A Living**

Includes finances, money,
vocation, even if you are
not paid: i.e. homemaker,
student, volunteer

STEP ONE MIND MAP
Part Two

Area of Unmanageability
Feeling of Uselessness

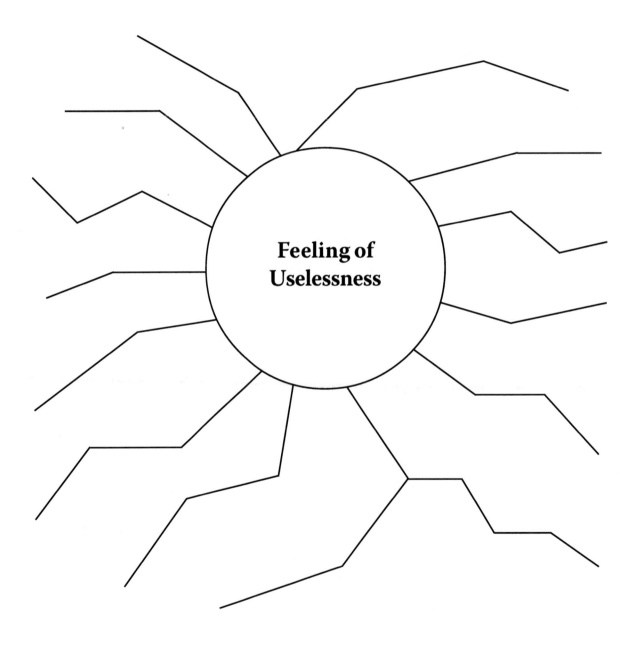

STEP ONE MIND MAP
Part Two

Area of Unmanageability
Full of Fear

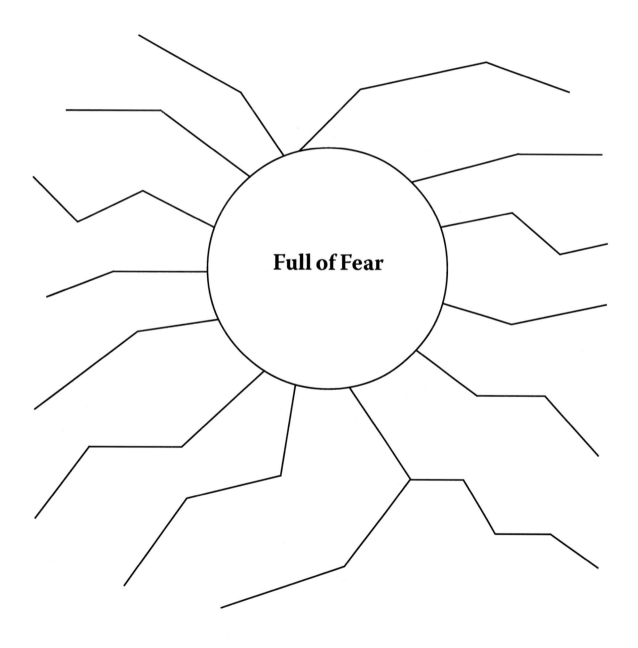

Full of Fear

STEP ONE MIND MAP
Part Two

Area of Unmanageability
We are Unhappy

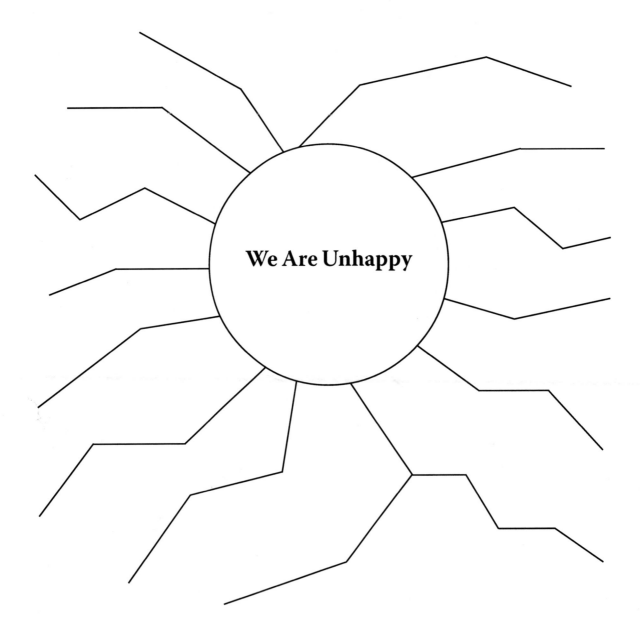

We Are Unhappy

STEP ONE MIND MAP
Part Two

Area of Unmanageability
Can't be of Real Help to Others

Can't be of Real Help to Others

"But seek first His Kingdom and His righteousness, and all these things will be given to you as well."
Matthew 6: 33

Chapter Two
Support for Step Two
Part One

O<small>N PAGE</small> 35 in *Alcoholics Anonymous* a man is described who, after a period of sobriety during which his life had begun to be repaired, drank again: "...(he) failed... to enlarge his spiritual life...". No matter how big our spiritual life may be, it must continue to grow.

"Quite as important was the discovery that spiritual principles would solve all my problems. I have since been brought into a way of living infinitely more satisfying and, I hope, more useful than the life I lived before." (page 42-43 in *Alcoholics Anonymous*) This was the promise and experience of one of A.A.'s early members.

Step Two is where dreams reawaken. It takes a little more time than Step One, but hang on for an incredible step. This step is in three parts. In the first, you will address and define the way your relationship with a Higher Power has or has not been working. You will face, during your writing, the Higher Power you have not trusted or believed in. Then, with the magic of your pen, you will ask yourself in writing: "What is the kind of Higher Power I am willing to trust, believe in, desire, or need, to bring about complete restoration in ALL areas of my life?" *This may be difficult.* It's hard to let go of old ideas. Any true maturity or growth involves questioning, discovery, growth and resolution. So write down the characteristics of a Higher Power you need. You have permission to write your heart's desire. What do you need this power to be to restore your life and help you to move into Step Three for a relationship? Think about entering any relationship. What are your "dream" characteristics for your "dream" God? A Higher Power, Spirit, Creator in a relationship where you matter and the restoration of your life matters.

The first time I did Part One with my 'old idea' of God it was easy. I had spent many years believing in a God that I did not trust completely, a God I resented and feared, a God who was critical and judgmental and required suffering and punishment. My distorted idea of God was, selective and exclusive, and I desperately sought approval by doing good works and trying to be perfect. I was afraid to recognize Him within my own being. Some of the words I wrote were: "I feel controlled, as if I don't matter; He only cares for the good or perfect. I can't really count on Him. He is a He and doesn't like women or need them for His service. He does not want the truth. He is punishing and judging, one-sided, and He expects too much of me; I have to be perfect before He is interested in helping or loving me."

You get the idea. Find out what is *not* working. Tell the truth. No matter what you think, this is about the old ideas and your feelings about a God you do not or cannot trust or believe in. Fears may surface as you write, voices from the past may whisper lies of betrayal. Write anyway, trusting this process, as many have gone before you and awakened with a God they could trust.

The next part of this step is to write out the *characteristics* of the kind of Higher Power that YOU need to restore your life, that you would be willing to trust.

Words like these may be used: "Higher Power likes me as Her creation; Higher Power clearly communicates. Higher Power is laughter, fun, joy, trust; I matter no matter what. He/She is trustworthy. ALL-powerful. Caring, creative, guidance is given. Higher Power can be counted on anytime—always available. He/She is a clear communicator. Love, creativity, beauty, compassion, forgiveness, understanding, is revealed in all of creation." What is your "heart's desire" for a Higher Power you can trust and believe in?

Warning here. I have found that as I allow the "dream" or the "hoped for" to enter my mind and heart it may hurt a little or a lot. I become vulnerable. And at the same time it feels good. I call this the "double-edged sword"—when the heart has been without love and feels as though it hasn't mattered and then becomes aware of how much love there is available, you may feel grief and happiness at the same time. Maybe it has been a long time since you thought of a Higher Power you wanted to be in relationship with, so this experience is like being reacquainted with a long-lost friend. You are about to rediscover yourself along with your Higher Power. So if it hurts and feels good at the same time, you are right on track. If not, these feelings may come later in the steps. Keep on going. You cannot do this step wrong as long as you remain honest, open-minded and willing. It gets better, I promise.

Chapter Two
STEP TWO
Part One

Came to believe that a power greater than ourselves could restore us to sanity.

*Restore—to take to a prior state of being
Sanity—soundness of mind*

📖 ***Read*** the chapter, "We Agnostics," pages 44-57 of *Alcoholics Anonymous*. Note the statement on page 55: "Sometimes we had to search fearlessly, but He was there. He was as much a fact as we were. We found the Great Reality deep down within us."

📖 ***Read*** the last paragraph on page 62 to the first paragraph on page 63 of *Alcoholics Anonymous*. Pay attention to the words "how" and "why," as well as the promises in these two paragraphs.

Ask yourself:
- Is it *possible* that a power greater than me exists that could bring about restoration within my being and in all areas in my life?
- If you are not able to believe, that is okay. Are you *willing* to believe?
- If you are *willing* to believe you will be asked to write down what characteristics God would have or be like *if* a Higher Power existed and could do these things.

Also, if you believe that there is no God, no Supreme Creator of life and at the same time you find yourself internally stirred with a mix of feelings as you reflect on this idea of God, you might consider this: it is difficult to be emotionally attached to someone or something that does not exist.

This step says God *could* restore me to sanity.
Am I *willing* to believe this *could* happen for me?

How big does God need to be to restore you and your life and help you solve your human problems?

PRINCIPLE **Willingness**

Chapter Two
STEP TWO
Part One (continued)

✍   *Complete a mind map of the characteristics of your old idea of God or a Power greater than you that you currently do not fully trust with all areas of your life. For those of you who do not believe in God, mind map the characteristics of a power greater than you that you do not trust, or the characteristics attributed to God that you do not believe in.*

✍   *Complete a mind map of the characteristics of a power greater than you, a Creator, Who could assist you in bringing about the desired changes in your life and that you would be willing to believe in and trust.*

PRINCIPLE *Willingness*

STEP TWO MIND MAP
Part One
Example

Characteristics of a Higher Power
Old Ideas

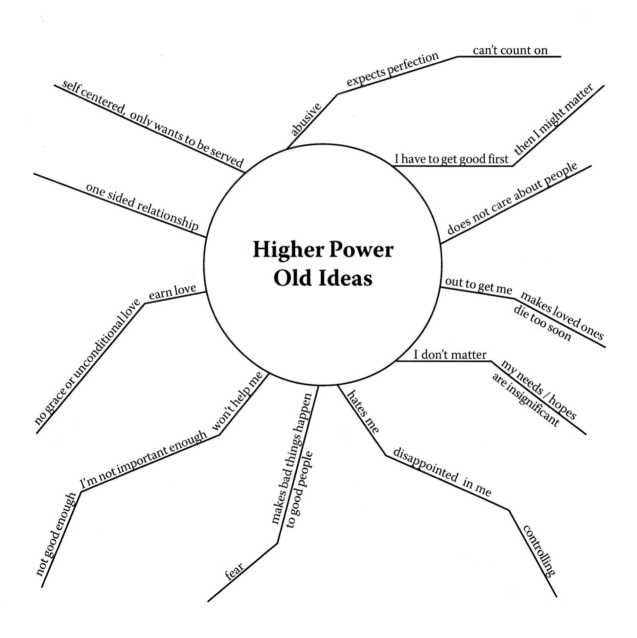

STEP TWO MIND MAP
Part One

Characteristics of a Higher Power
Your Old Ideas

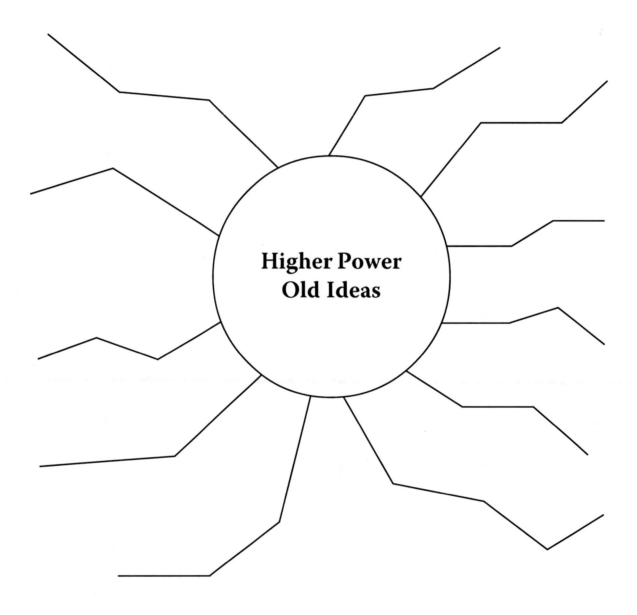

STEP TWO MIND MAP
Part One
Example

Characteristics of a Higher Power
New Ideas

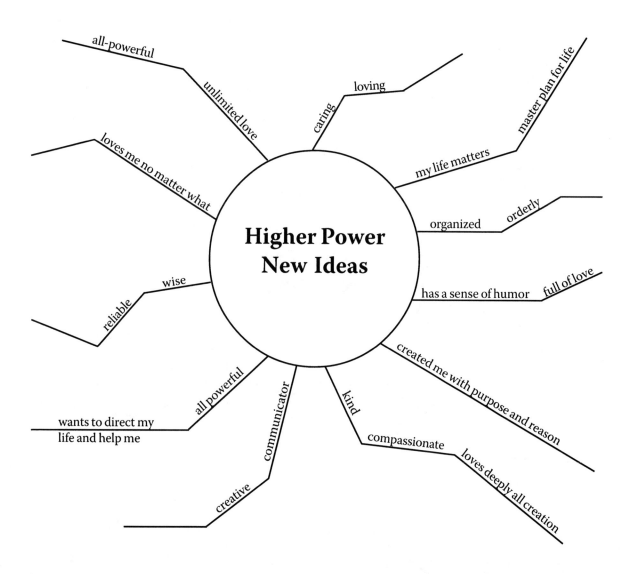

STEP TWO MIND MAP
Part One

Characteristics of a Higher Power
Your New Ideas

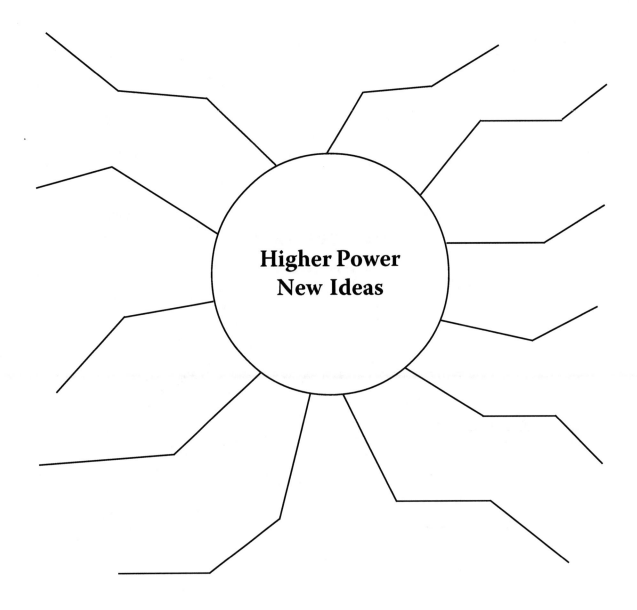

Chapter Two
Support for Step Two
Part Two

THE NINE AREAS that you will now be asked to write about for your restoration may be more difficult than Step One. I argued years ago about the word "restore" in this step. I could not recall a time in my life to which I wanted to be restored, so I thought this word was a mistake. A kind person asked me to reflect on what I see with a newborn baby, thinking that would help. A baby is trusting, precious, and asks for what it needs, so a baby is honest. And oh, an infant is full of wonder, each new day. With this guidance I became willing to believe in my restoration and desire to be restored.

Some of us have spent too much mental and emotional energy thinking and looking at what is wrong in ourselves and our lives. We are unhappy, yet misery for some can be more comfortable than happiness. Step Two visioning requires a willingness to reflect and try to remember some of the dreams held in our hearts. Without judgment or fear, try to recall the "who" you wanted to be or the "who" you desire to become. It may help to take your writing from Step One and ask yourself, "What is the opposite of each area of unmanageability?" "What would it be like if I or my life were restored?" Just write the opposite of Step One mind maps. Use words and phrases in your mind map for your hope and dreams for restoration. Examples are to follow, but the important thing is to write down your heart's desire. Go for it; 'shoot for the moon.' Let go of the old ideas about who you are and who you were supposed to be. Discover your dreams. Let the words flow. You may borrow any idea, if it is right for you. I had to borrow dreams from others when I first began, as cultural and generational ideas were limiting my hopes and dreams.

My sense of having the right to restoration and purpose, bliss, joy and even to having a savings account was shaky. You don't have to believe it possible, just write down your heart's desire. Even if it is a few words on some of the mind maps, that is a great start.

Remember when you were a little kid and who you wanted to be when you grew up would change from one week to the next? You dreamed of being the President, a ballerina or scientist, or even a rock and roll singer or famous artist. Remember those days of being *willing* to dream? Well, today there is no one who has the authority to tell you what your heart's desire looks like. So go for it! You may find this part may hurt (it hurt me to realize how long it had been since I had been free to dream), but you must trust your right to dream again. A certain vulnerability is necessary for you to reveal first to yourself what your heart's desire looks like, leaving shame behind, and then to share this with another trusted person. You may find this work more difficult than Step One but do not let old ideas or shame rob you of your right to dream again.

Allow the words to flow, stopping any mental analysis of the probability of your dreams coming true. This step is about reclaiming your heart's desire.

How are you going to recognize being restored to sanity if you have no idea of what it looks like?

Can God's efforts go unrecognized?

Reach out and stretch with this step, no matter how you may feel. Pretend it is a "dream step" if need be. This is not the time to shortchange yourself in writing, so go ahead and claim your heart's desire in all areas. Whether it looks big or small to others does not matter. It may look impossible—it does not matter. Write down your desires, hopes and dreams. What would you do or become if nothing and no one held you back? Look at other people's lives: who do you admire? Look for examples to help get you started.

Also, an *old idea* may surface at this time: "we should just be grateful for being where we are and what we have." I have found that this indicates a lazy or fearful spirit. And that too is okay if that is what you choose. (Or you can release this old idea and write your hopes, dreams and inspirations for your life.)

God calls each of us to serve Creator-Spirit, as well as our fellows, once we are fully alive. If I do not look beyond my old ideas of who I think I am or who I think I am 'supposed' to be, with courage and fearless efforts, to uncover who God created me to be—no matter what stage of life I may presently be in—I will be destined to spend many dark hours alone, bitterly wondering what might have been.

Remember – nothing is too big—Dream again!

Chapter Two
STEP TWO
Part Two

📖   ***Read*** page 63 and take note of the promise at the end of Step Two, the last three words before Step Three are, "We were reborn."

*Step Two asserts the idea, hope and promise of being restored to Sanity. Dreams and hopes can be as big as you are **willing** to let them be.*

This is where we remember what it was like to dream unashamed. With the openness of a small child, the wonder of a heart unafraid, give written form to the desires of your life.

Ask yourself as you write your mind maps:
- What would each area look like if God restored you/your life to sanity?
- What are your hopes and dreams in each area?

✍   ***Complete a mind map with your desire, vision, dream and hope, for each of the nine areas of unmanageability, for God to restore. Be specific and use plenty of adjectives that describe your vision, include feeling words!***

✍   ***Complete a vision statement for each of the nine areas using words from each mind map. Write affirmatively, that is: "I am...", "Today I experience...".****

❋ *Save these pages for review after all of the steps have been completed.*

You cannot do this part wrong, but please write out your dreams and desires *as if* they have already been achieved. Write your statements in the present tense, "I am." One area of restoration may have one sentence and another area may require a full page and some areas may look similar to each other. Try to do only three mind maps at a given time, to allow new ideas to spring forth.

How are you going to recognize your spiritual awakening and being restored to sanity and a manageable life if you don't know what it "looks" like?

Don't let your awakening go by unrecognized by you!

PRINCIPLE *Willingness*

43

STEP TWO MIND MAP
Part Two
Example

Area of Restoration
Personal Relationships

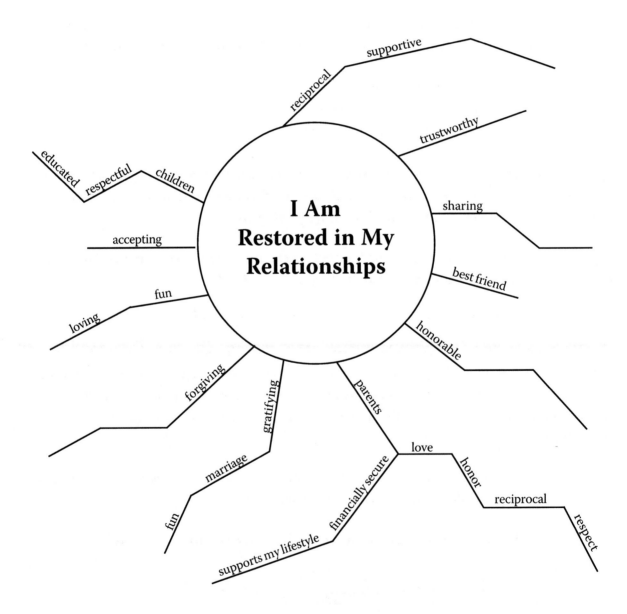

STEP TWO VISION STATEMENT
Part Two
Example

Area of Restoration
Personal Relationships

Save this page for review after all of the steps have been completed.

My relationships are forgiving, fun, loving and accepting. I experience recipro-cal support and honor. My relationships are trustworthy, as I am trustworthy and I use good judgment to discern who is trustworthy. I honor behavior that is honorable. I treat my parents with honor and respect, setting boundaries that allow me to grow as the person I am.

There is room in my life for the growth and change that is taking place so that I feel secure in my humanity. My friends support my growth as I support them. I have time alone and time with family and friends that is fun and memo-rable. I create new traditions with those I love that celebrate life. I participate in family traditions that I enjoy and see how my participation adds to the lives of others.

STEP TWO MIND MAP
Part Two

Area of Restoration
Personal Relationships

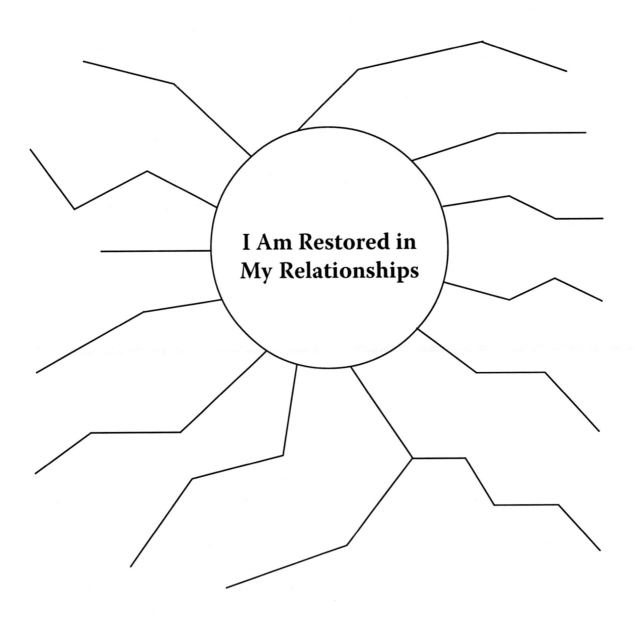

I Am Restored in
My Relationships

STEP TWO VISION STATEMENT
Part Two

Area of Restoration
Personal Relationships

Take words from your mind map to write your vision statement for the area of personal relationships. Write in the affirmative as though the desired state has already come to pass, i.e., "I am..." or "I experience today..." An example could be, "I am free to participate in intimate relationships as I honor myself, others and seek the good within all people. I give myself freedom to choose who I spend time with each day and nurture reciprocal relationships, including my relationship with God." Save this page for review after all of the steps have been completed.

I am restored in the area of my relationships...........
_____
_____
_____
_____
_____
_____
_____
_____
_____
_____
_____
_____
_____
_____
_____
_____
_____
_____
_____
_____
_____
_____

STEP TWO MIND MAP
Part Two

Area of Restoration
Emotional Nature

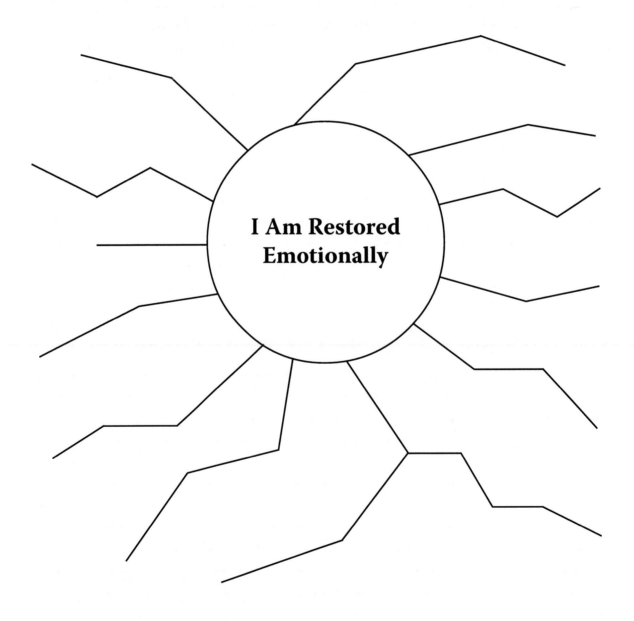

I Am Restored
Emotionally

STEP TWO VISION STATEMENT
Part Two

Area of Restoration
Emotional Nature

Take words from your mind map to write your vision statement for the area of your emotional nature. Write affirmatively: "I am..." or "I experience today...". Example: "My emotional nature is balanced and harmonious as I spend time each day in prayer and meditation. Whenever I am disturbed I quickly look within to find calm. I freely express my emotions and honor this aspect of my human nature, no longer blaming others or situations for my feelings. Today I experience freedom as a human and spiritual being."

Save this page for review after all of the steps have been completed.

I am restored emotionally................

_____

_____

_____

_____

_____

_____

_____

_____

_____

_____

_____

_____

_____

_____

_____

_____

_____

_____

_____

_____

_____

STEP TWO MIND MAP
Part Two

Area of Restoration
Freedom from Misery

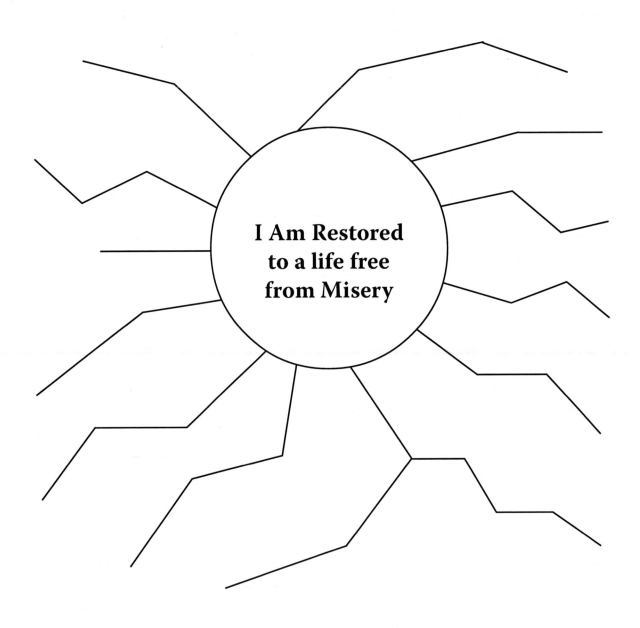

**I Am Restored
to a life free
from Misery**

STEP TWO VISION STATEMENT
Part Two

Area of Restoration
Freedom from Misery

Take words from your mind map to write your vision statement for the area of freedom from misery. Write affirmatively, as if describing a change that has taken place: "I am..." or "I experience today...". Example: "I'm not controlled by misery—it is simply an occasional emotion that I feel, express and release!"

Save this page for review after all of the steps have been completed.

I am restored and free from misery.........

_____

_____

_____

_____

_____

_____

_____

_____

_____

_____

_____

_____

_____

_____

_____

_____

_____

_____

_____

_____

_____

_____

_____

_____

STEP TWO MIND MAP
Part Two

Area of Restoration
Freedom from Depression

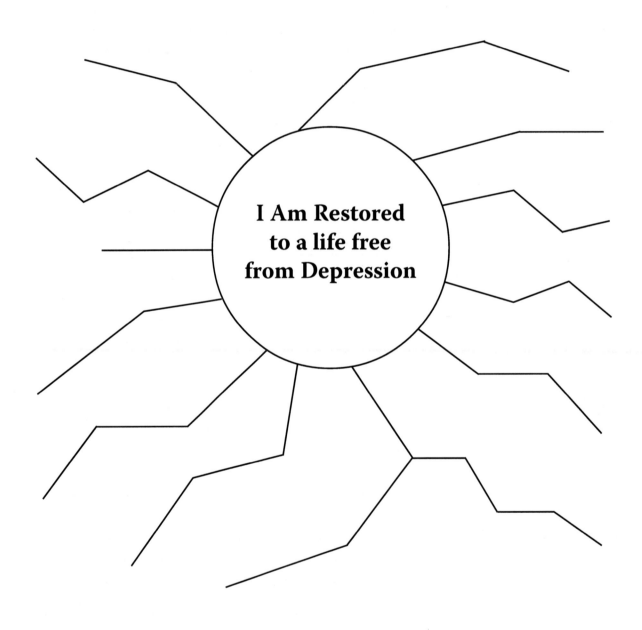

I Am Restored to a life free from Depression

STEP TWO VISION STATEMENT
Part Two

Area of Restoration
Freedom from Depression

Take words from your mind map to write your vision statement for this area, freedom from depression. Write in the affirmative: "I am...", "Today I experience...". Example: "I have balanced emotions and when depression fills my heart, I share it and let go. If not, then I seek help to resolve depression as an emotion, and not as the center of my existence." Or "I freely express my anger in appropriate ways and with safe and trustworthy people, and depression no longer controls my actions." Save this page for review after all of the steps have been completed.

I am restored and free from depression............... _____

_____

_____

_____

_____

_____

_____

_____

_____

_____

_____

_____

_____

_____

_____

_____

STEP TWO MIND MAP
Part Two

Area of Restoration
Make a Living

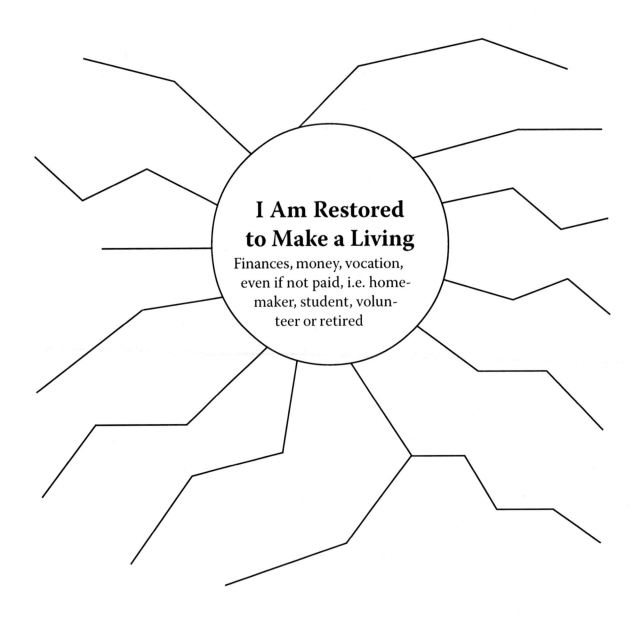

**I Am Restored
to Make a Living**
Finances, money, vocation,
even if not paid, i.e. homemaker, student, volun-
teer or retired

STEP TWO VISION STATEMENT
Part Two

Area of Restoration
Make a Living

Take words from your mind map to write your vision statement for this area, for making a living (or as a student, homemaker, etc.). Write in the affirmative: "I am...," "I experience today...". Example: "I confidently and joyfully express my passion in my work and completing school is now a priority." "I have money saved to complete my education as I honor the process of learning." "My purpose unfolds as I trust each step of the way."

Save this page for review after all of the steps have been completed.

I am restored in the area of money, finances, work, school, my vocation, household responsibilities.................

_____

_____

_____

_____

_____

_____

_____

_____

_____

_____

_____

_____

_____

_____

_____

_____

_____

_____

_____

_____

_____

_____

STEP TWO MIND MAP
Part Two

Area of Restoration
Feelings of Usefulness

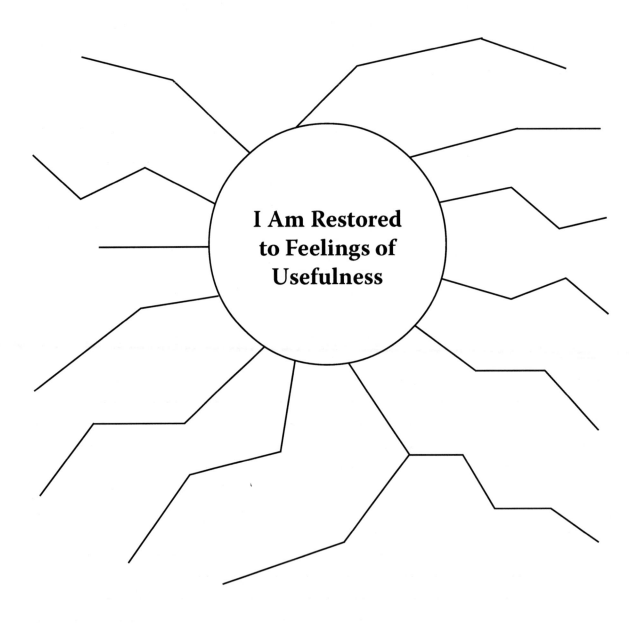

Chapter Two

STEP TWO VISION STATEMENT
Part Two

Area of Restoration
Feelings of Usefulness

Take words from your mind map to write your vision statement for being restored to feelings of usefulness. Write affirmatively: "I am...", "I experience today...". Example: "I am useful in many areas of my life, I take care of my house plants and the garden I have created, and I enjoy this." "I am useful as I offer rides to the elderly each day I attend Church." "I am useful and experience the feeling that there are plenty of hours each day to achieve my purposes, and I feel satisfied in my use of the time given me."

Save this page for review after all of the steps have been completed.

*I am restored to usefulness..........*_____

_____

_____

_____

_____

STEP TWO MIND MAP
Part Two

Area of Restoration
Free from Fear

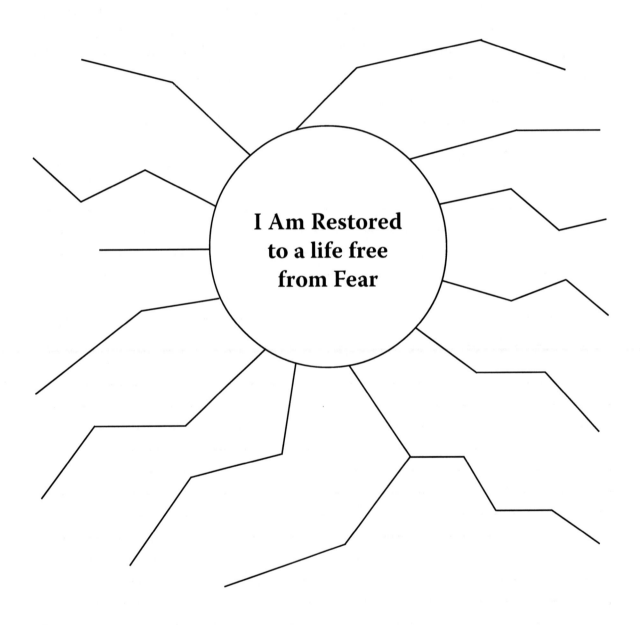

**I Am Restored
to a life free
from Fear**

STEP TWO VISION STATEMENT
Part Two

Area of Restoration
Free from Fear

Take words from your mind map to write your vision statement to reflect your freedom from fear. Affirm your vision with the present tense: "I am...", "I experience today...". Example: "I embrace the fears that have held me hostage and I am no longer controlled by fear. I accept fear as an emotion that comes with being human and each time I recognize I am afraid, I gently remind myself of the solutions to fear." Save this page for review after all of the steps have been completed.

I am restored to live free from fear, I am........ _____

_____

_____

_____

_____

_____

_____

_____

_____

_____

_____

_____

_____

_____

_____

_____

_____

_____

_____

_____

_____

STEP TWO MIND MAP
Part Two

Area of Restoration
Happiness

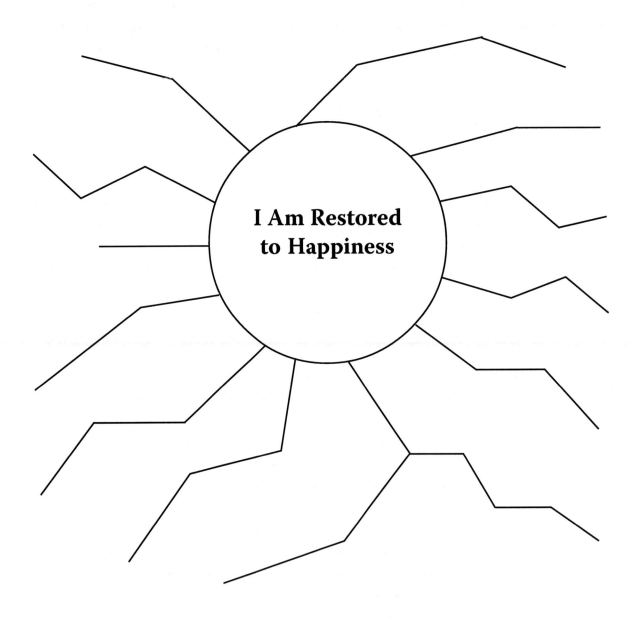

Chapter Two

STEP TWO VISION STATEMENT
Part Two

Area of Restoration
Happiness

Take words from your mind map to write your vision statement for this area as you are restored to happiness. Write in the affirmative: "I am...", "I experience today...". Example: "I am happy and at peace with the unique person I was created to be. I applaud my efforts each day as I practice being fully alive as the human spiritual being I was created to be. When unhappiness comes I acknowledge the emotion, examine it, and share the experience with those I trust, treating myself with gentle care."

Save this page for review after all of the steps have been completed.

I am restored and now experience happiness..........

_____

_____

_____

_____

_____

_____

_____

_____

_____

_____

_____

_____

_____

_____

_____

_____

_____

_____

_____

STEP TWO MIND MAP
Part Two

Area of Restoration
Real Help to Others

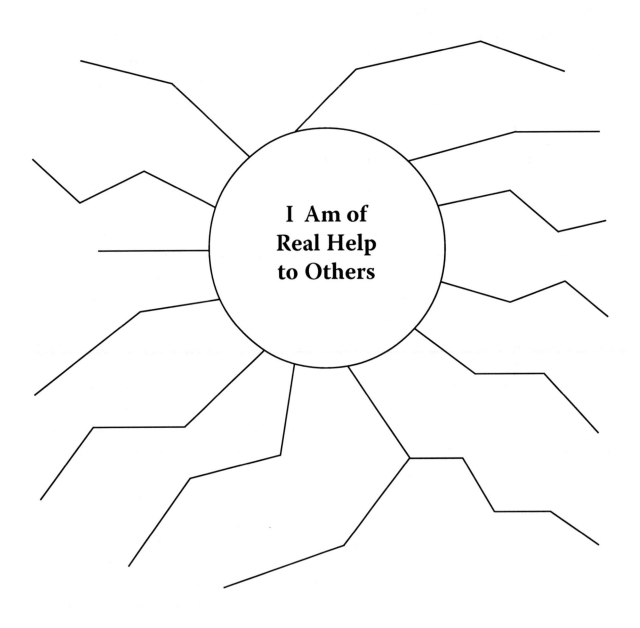

I Am of
Real Help
to Others

STEP TWO VISION STATEMENT
Part Two

Area of Restoration
Real Help to Others

Take words from your mind map to write your vision statement for this area as you are restored to being of real help to others. Write in the affirmative: "I am...", "I experience today...". Example: "I help others each new day, I reach out and find ways to support single parents to become educated. Today I am a participant in society, looking for solutions and not just problems."

Save this page for review after all of the steps have been completed.

I am restored and I am now of real help to others........

_____

_____

_____

_____

_____

_____

_____

_____

_____

_____

_____

_____

_____

_____

_____

_____

_____

_____

_____

_____

_____

_____

*"So I say to you: Ask and it will be given to you; Seek and you will find;
knock and the door will be opened to you.
For everyone who asks receives; he who seeks finds;
and to him who knocks, the door will be opened."*
Luke 11: 9-10

Chapter Three
Support for Step Three

THIS STEP SEEMED EASIER when I was clear in my own mind that it was about entering a *relationship* with God. Too many times I had made a decision to surrender my life to God's care and then wondered why nothing changed. I offered myself to Him many times in my youth, yet the giving of myself was always followed by great disappointment. It was as though I had the mind of a child, looking for magic! It was as if I were waiting to be tapped on the head with a magic wand—then to wake up and see that I had been restored, renewed, and become someone I could live with.

Never had I seen that it was a relationship I was entering—by choice—where I had a part and Creator/Spirit had a part. I had to let go of the idea that God was a tyrant master and I was a helpless puppet. I had to do things different if I wanted previously written changes to occur. I needed to play a significant part in this relationship. I put on paper what I needed a relationship with my Higher Power to "look like." I described a relationship to which I would commit myself. As a basis of comparison I thought of the dating that leads to marriage. What characteristics do you expect in a relationship that make you want it to continue, that make you want it to become a life-changing commitment?

Writing this step was liberating for me and gave me hope. Could I have this kind of relationship with my Creator? That was the desire of my heart: a working relationship that would hold together through any challenge. A relationship I could depend on, no matter what! Spirit would never leave and I would follow, for this was a relationship I was willing to trust, based on love and commitment.

This was also a time when I got rid of a lot of old ideas about who God was and who I was as a spiritual woman. You may find your old ideas coming up at this time as well. I pushed past the old ideas (they did not work anyway) and I did mind maps of a relationship for God and me. The first time I did this I was able to write down five words. The second time I used this technique I filled a page with words about my desired relationship. Some of the things I wrote were, "I honor God as my Creator—I am honored by God as His/Her creation, I experience clear communication, laughter, fun, joy, intimacy, purpose, trust. I can trust God to lead and God can trust me to follow." These are a few of the ideas I used and today I have just such a relationship with God.

Willingness is essential in this step. Are you willing to reveal your desired relationship with Creator? With no judgment as to right or wrong, are you willing to simply reveal your heart's desire? If not, you can pray and ask for the willingness until it comes. Better yet, if fear is stopping you at this point, ask someone that you trust and respect to describe their relationship with God and "borrow" their idea until you have the courage to reveal your own.

Deep within is the wellspring of the endless presence of God.

Chapter Three
STEP THREE

*Made a decision to turn our will and life over to the
care of God as we understood Him.*

📖   **Read** pages 58-63 of *Alcoholics Anonymous*, paying special attention to the last paragraph on page 62 that ends on the top of page 63. A relationship with God is described—both Gods' part and my part. In this relationship both parties will take an active role.

What is your heart's desire for your relationship with Divine Spirit?

What does Creator's part and your part in the relationship look like?

✒   **Complete a mind map of what you want your relationship with God to look like (to which you can entrust your will and life).**

✒   **Write a vision statement, using words from this mind map, describing the relationship you desire to enter with God, including both His role and yours.***

📖   **Read and share your vision statement with a trusted person and pray the Third Step prayer, found on page 63 in Alcoholics Anonymous. A trusted person may be a sponsor, group, minister, friend or family member.**

Save this page for review after all of the steps have been completed.

Third Step Prayer

"God, I offer myself to Thee – to build with me and to do with me as Thou wilt. Relieve me of the bondage of self, that I may better do Thy will. Take away my difficulties, that victory over them may bear witness to those I may help of Thy Power, Thy Love, and Thy Way of life. May I do Thy will always!"

PRINCIPLE *Faith*

STEP THREE MIND MAP
Example

My Relationship with God/Creator

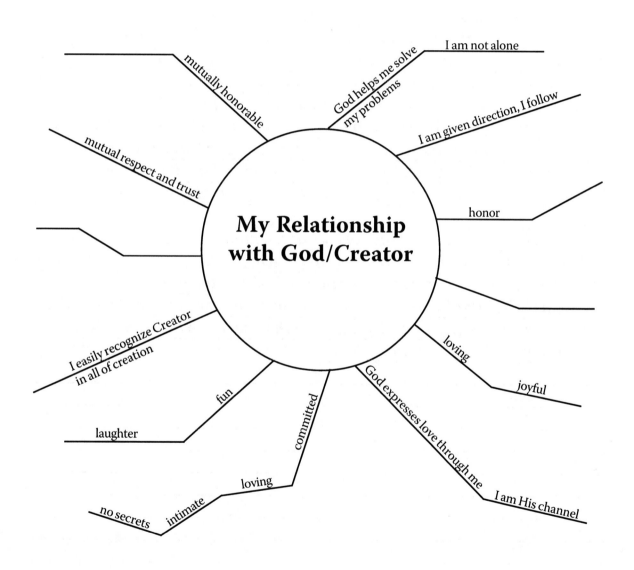

STEP THREE VISION STATEMENT
Example

My Relationship with God/Creator
Save this page for review after all of the steps have been completed.

My relationship with Creator is one that is based in trust and honor. God honors me as His/Her creation and I honor Him/Her as my Creator. I speak words of love and respect when reflecting on this relationship. We have time daily set aside to be alone with each other, to grow in intimacy and love for one another. I trust the guidance I receive from Spirit and the evidence and direction that are supplied to keep me on course. I am a disciplined spirit and can be trusted, as I trust. I matter in this relationship and all my needs are met and provided for—I follow God's leading. I am committed to this relationship and God is committed to me as the One with all power to assist in solving and helping me with my problems and shortcomings. I trust Creator with my loved ones as well. This is a delightful and, at times, humorous relationship as it is awkward and we laugh. God reflects His presence in life surrounding me and in the silence. I share freely my adoration of God and the Holy Spirit and I am free from the spiritual shame carried since my youth for my love of God. With ease I share this precious relationship with those who are interested. I love my relationship with God/Creator, whose Spirit will never leave me – ever!

STEP THREE MIND MAP

My Relationship with God/Creator

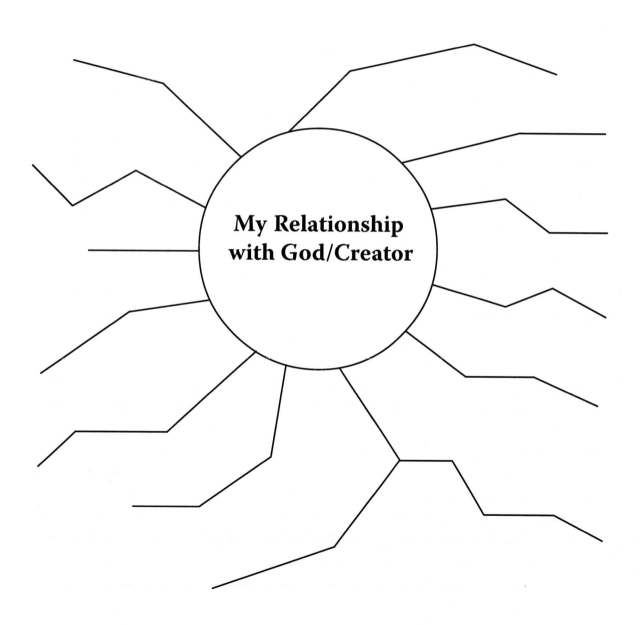

STEP THREE VISION STATEMENT

My Relationship with God/Creator
Save this page for review after all of the steps have been completed.

My relationship with God/Creator/Spirit is.......... _____

_____

_____

_____

_____

_____

_____

_____

_____

_____

_____

_____

_____

_____

_____

_____

_____

_____

_____

_____

_____

_____

_____

"There is nothing concealed that will not be disclosed, or hidden that will not be made known."
Luke 12: 2

Chapter Four
Support for Step Four

Begin Step Four by taking a deep breath and praying for the willingness to take the action required to cement your newfound relationship with God. The purpose of the Fourth Step is to look at and inventory what isn't working in your life. I had never really told a single person the whole truth about a situation or about myself before I did my first written inventory. I had been too afraid of what would be thought of me, or worse yet, what would happen to me if anyone found out the me I *thought* I was. I had believed I was nothing and at other times thought too much of myself. This step gave me an opportunity to look at information in black and white, and on paper. In the process I was able to recognize what had prevented me from being the person I was created to be.

The Fourth Step is not about looking for the things that are right about us. It is an inventory of those things that have been kept hidden from the light of Gods' grace. To bring about freedom, complete honesty is necessary with this step. This is not the time to try to make our thoughts, actions or experiences look nice, nor is it the time to pass judgment on others or ourselves. We are simply taking inventory—gathering information. For those who have not taken such a look before, this step may take some time, and a lot of courage, as well as support from your trusted support person.

I have written a number of inventories, and remember wondering at the time what was meant in Step Five about the "exact nature" of my wrongs. Following the procedures I have set forth in this workbook, I was able see that the exact nature of my wrongs was the perception I had formed and retained in my mind about occurrences in my life. Thus the actions I took or decisions I made were based on misperceptions about who I was—and how I was—as well as who and how you were. It hurt me to see this. It made me sad to see how many decisions I had made based on incorrect information.

Painful though it may be, this step is necessary to have a Spiritual Awakening. To awaken to my divine nature, I first had to look at what was keeping me from God's grace. I had to face the ugliest parts of my character and take a hard look at the times I had misused the human power given to me. I had to face the fact that at some time in my life, to varying degrees, I had misused all my powers.

Over time survival is no longer a justification for our defects. We hold on to them and trust them like a shield of armor. Fear has turned to anger, rage or depression and we rely upon these states like weapons for protection. Sadly, by the time we get around to writing this inventory we begin to realize that the same defects that once helped us to get by or get ahead are now the very things in our character that are keeping us from experiencing any true form of happiness or partnership with others.

All of us have been given power. Physical, emotional, spiritual, sexual, mental abilities and financial means. It is in misusing or denying our abilities and gifts that our hearts are brought the deepest pain and loneliness. By honestly looking at the misuse of our powers we have the hope of coming into harmony with our Creator and properly using all of our gifts, talents and powers. A disciplined spirit is one God can count on to properly use these gifts. However, first it is necessary to admit the misuse of one's powers.

Stay in close contact with your support person and remember: this is a gathering of information— not the gathering of testimony for a final judgment of who you are. You must bring to light those things that are keeping you from being the authentic you that God created you to be. Yet this information-gathering is an important step that can't be skipped. Before you have finished writing your Fourth Step you will be surprised by some of what you discover, and I hope comforted to know you are not alone as you write. This step is faith in action.

Chapter Four
STEP FOUR

Made a searching and fearless moral inventory of ourselves.

📖   ***Read*** thoroughly pages 63-71 in *Alcoholics Anonymous.*

"Next we launched out on a course of vigorous action, the first step of which is a personal housecleaning, which many of us had never attempted...So we had to get down to causes and conditions." (page 63 in *Alcoholics Anonymous*)

✱*A separate notebook will be needed for the Fourth Step writing. This writing in particular is to be kept in a private and secure place, where no one can find it and read it, or be tempted to do so.*

🖎   **Complete a resentment inventory - Part One.**
    Section One - Column I, II and III
    Section Two - Column IV and V

🖎   **Complete a fear inventory - Part Two.**
    Section One - List of Fears
    Section Two - Solution to Fears

🖎   **Complete a sex inventory - Part Three.**
    Section One - What Did They Do?
    Section Two - What Did I Do?
    Section Three - Future Sex Life

Please keep in mind that it is not a prerequisite for you to suffer or become depressed while writing this inventory. Emotions will arise, but suffering is not necessary. Keep in mind at all times that this is simply a look at what within your life is no longer working, so it may be released. This release will allow you tremendous freedom in later steps.

PRINCIPLE
Rigorous Honesty, Willingness and Trust

Chapter Four
Support for Resentment Inventory

In order to see our own defects or faults it is first necessary to write down what "they" did – with no need to prove or judge. Your false ego – the one holding you hostage to old ways of thinking and living, is afraid it will die or become nothing – given this opportunity, will free your true ego self – to flourish.

BEFORE WRITING it may be helpful to pray, asking God for guidance and inspiration, so that you will trust your effort of honesty, as you write the names of persons, institutions and principles. Follow this order in writing: pray first and with a separate and private journal or notebook, write a list of names that come to mind – this becomes your Column I. It is important to trust your efforts in writing this list, and trust that they are connected to some past hurt regarding something that happened or something that did not happen. I have found that when I pray, trusting God to help me be as honest as I can to write this list, I have been able to recall the resentments or hurts connected with each name, institution or principle. There is no need to be concerned about leaving off someone, with no intent, as more inventories will come, and anyone left out of this inventory will come to mind when it is the perfect and supportive time to face such hurts. We simply need to be as honest as we can be, at this time, trusting new days bring new awareness! Withholding anything that you judge to be insignificant, is not an honest and thorough inventory, if an incident or situation has held onto your consciousness, then it is worthy of noting in this part of your inventory. The last section of this inventory may be a more accurate place to write about another's action; institution or principle as it is related to our sexual identity, if you have no part associated with this.

After writing your list, Column I, and you have a good feeling that this is complete, it is time to move towards writing Column II. If you are uncertain if this list is not complete, remembering we are not striving for perfection, but an honest inventory, then set this aside for a few hours or a new day to allow your mind to return to the inventory with a refreshed mind. For anyone who has written inventories before and you find the same names or institutions on your resentment list again, then trust there is more to discover about the resentment and this process will support you toward freedom from the past. It has also been helpful for me to number the list of names, institutions or principles, to refer too when writing in Column II. Sometimes there is more than one incident to write about in Column II for one name in Column I.

Column II, is the place to write what 'they' did or what 'they' failed to do. This is a time to be as specific as you can be and also the chance to write, "What am I mad about?" Withholding nothing, no matter how trivial or insignificant it may seem at this time. Write down everything, every incident when you were angry, hurt or upset about something that happened or did not happen. This is not the time to prove or justify anything. If it is your reality, it is real. What did they do or not do? Write something for each person, institution or principle from Column I.

I have found it more difficult, at times, to define principles associated with resentments or hurts, than personalities or institutions. Taking a principle from your Column I, and consider the hurts from trying to live by this principle or the hurts from being judged by the principle you resent. A few ideas of principles are listed in the examples in the following pages. Some things to consider as you list your hurts from principles, is to think how this principle adversely impacted you. And what supported the principle that you came to resent? How did you learn this principle and what are you angry about? You will continue to use a separate notebook for the inventory section of this process. One last thought about principles, is it may be something you believe in, a principle you hoped to live according too, and the anger is over failing to live up to your own expectations. Any resentment over a principle would also include a time when I think I am accountable to an acceptable principle and appearances tell me that others are not held to the same standards. This is a time to write about your anger, hurt or bitterness.

Praying before moving into Column III was necessary for me to have the needed courage and strength to write truthfully and thoroughly. For those persons, institutions or principles that I still feel resentful towards, I pray for them, recognizing they too are spiritually sick, and I will not give them the power to keep me from becoming who God created me to be.

I have found it beneficial to ask God to forgive those that I can not - through me,
although I may still be angry or hurt, I ask God to forgive others as I hope to be forgiven.
I pray and ask to be a channel for Gods forgiveness.

Focusing on Column III, referring to the numbers associated with each name and specifically the *numbered resentments* in Column II, this is the place to write a detailed account, answering questions outlined in the directions page to discover "why am I angry." This also includes feelings of hurt, guilt, shame, etc. My first effort in writing 'why I was angry' was not difficult. It became harder when I was asked what my beliefs or ideas about who men are or who men are supposed to be or who women are or who women are expected to be, in my inventory with Column III. I had a difficult time becoming aware of my perceptions, and sometimes misperceptions of a given situation – and these arise in our resentments, our perception or what happened to make us angry. It required much effort in writing Column III, and I was able to answer a haunting question that had been with me for years. *What was the exact nature of my wrongs?* I had read in *Alcoholics Anonymous*, that the problem of the alcoholic centers in the mind. I had completed numerous inventories and this question had never been answered or resolved, until I gave myself the time to answer the questions, for each resentment in Column III.

It is in this column that I discovered old ideas and beliefs that had become the basis for my daily living. I had taken on the beliefs of those who did not reflect my spirit, such as, 'women are not to be trusted and they are competitive." Another old idea I uncovered was, "only men can be good artists", this belief came from my perception of a resentment I had when I was 10 years old. But, I lived and acted out this old idea. I felt women were competitive at work and then when my children would bring their school art home, I would unconsciously display and frame my son's art and then I would encourage my daughter to write. Old ideas are not always accurate, as both my children are creative and talented. Once I was aware that I was still living and acting out this misperception I was able to make amends to my children. Looking at who was hurt by me and amends owed comes later in the steps.

It is in Column III that you will recognize your old ideas and beliefs, and see why you need a psychic change. Here I was able to discover the foundation for the beliefs that drove my character defects, sustained my hurtful behavior, and caused my mistakes. I was finally able to see the *exact nature of my wrongs*, and filled with courage I was able to face beliefs and prejudices that I had acted upon.

Answer the questions in Column III and write your perceptions and beliefs as it relates to your self-esteem, personal relationships, sex relations, ambitions, security and pocketbook, basically, "who I think I am" in each area, this is not a simple yes or no answer. Answer the questions as it relates to every resentment you have listed in Column II. *This may take some time,* but a thorough inventory will uncover root causes and allow you to pass into a freedom that goes to your soul. I was able to uncover who I am and let go of my hurtful actions that were based on inaccurate perceptions, ideas or beliefs. This is not a short cut, but I have found this part, Column III to be a very necessary action to discover those very things that have been hidden from my consciousness and demanded that I live bitterly. I wanted freedom from the past and my resentments, this came at the price of my time and effort in Column III.

Exposing these harbored resentments, actions and feelings to the light of the Spirit will allow healing and soul freedom.

This is when my soul began to dance again, as I could hear the rhythm of the song deep within my heart.

Chapter Four
STEP FOUR RESENTMENT INVENTORY
Part One - Section One - Column I, II and III

Pray, before you begin writing your inventory.

"God, thank you for the gift of honesty and willingness that has brought me to this point in my spiritual growth. Your grace is necessary for me to fearlessly write an honest list of persons, institutions or principles that I have resentments towards. I ask for courage, honesty, and grace to write this inventory and to see this as an avenue for me to live free, as my most authentic self." Amen

✻ *Remember to write your inventory in one private notebook.*

✒ **Column I - The List:** *Write, after praying, a list of people, institutions and principles of those you have resentments toward. Number each one for later reference.*

This list includes **persons**, **institutions** and **principles** that have caused you *resentments*.

The list of *Persons* may include individuals or groups of people. This may include loved ones, God, self, friends, persons you no longer recall their name, loved ones who have died, family members, or groups of people such as: all men, all women, all children, all addicts or alcoholics, all those married or divorced, those convicted of crimes, the elderly, all doctors, all ministers, the handicapped, persons who are wealthy, the poor, the chronically ill, caregivers for the ill, those who receive financial or medical assistance from the government, or politicians.

The list of *Institutions* may include the IRS, medical community, military, government at the Federal, State or City level, lawyers, governing bodies, schools, religion, non-profit organizations or other business'.

The list of *Principles* may include ideas, beliefs, rules or expectations. •Some of these principles could be from your family, religion or media, or unspoken rules you are expected to live by; such as 'men do not cry', 'I am stupid', 'it is not okay to take off from work', etc. It might be helpful to refer to the Introduction that discuss' 'old ideas' as principles you resent.

When writing your list of resentments, trust this process, even if you can not recall at this time what resentment is connected to each person – this awareness will come later.

Rigorous Honesty, Willingness and Trust

Chapter Four
STEP FOUR RESENTMENT INVENTORY
Part One - Section One - Column I, II and III (continued)

✍ *Column II - The Cause: From the list in Column I, starting with number one on your list, write what you resent, asking yourself what did 'they' do or what did 'they' fail to do. Write down each situation or issue that causes you resentment before going on to the next name on your list, and so on, until you have written your resentments for each name, institution and principle.*

You may find some names from Column I that may have more than one resentment or situation to write about, and some names will have only one resentment associated with that particular person, institution or principle.

✍ *Column III - "Why Am I angry?": Write, asking yourself the following questions, for each resentment or situation you have listed in Column II.*

Why Am I angry? Does this situation hurt, threaten or interfere with my:

Self – Esteem: What does this situation tell me about my perception or belief, about who I think I am or who I think I should be?

Personal Relations : What does this situation tell me about my perception or belief, about who I think I am or who I think I should be, as well as who I think others are or who they should be?

Sex Relations: What does this situation tell me about my perception or belief, about who I think men, women are supposed to be or who they should be regarding sex and sexuality?

Ambitions: What does this situation tell me about my perception or belief about who I think I am, who I should be or who I want to be? What did I desire, want or hope for in regards to myself, others or my community, culture or family?

PRINCIPLE

Rigorous Honesty, Willingness and Trust

Chapter Four
STEP FOUR RESENTMENT INVENTORY
Part One - Section One - Column I, II and III (continued)

Security: What does this situation tell me about my perception or belief about who I think I am or who I should be, and who I wanted to be, needed, hoped for or desired?

Pocketbook: What does this situation tell me about my perception or belief about who I think I am or who I think I should be, regarding money and my vocation; as a business owner, employee, homemaker, spouse, parent, child, student or volunteer. What did I want, need, hope for or desire?

Column III does takes time – try not to stop at this phase of your work.

This inventory will become easier, after completing Column III. It is in this column that we discover our old ideas and the misuse of our powers, and begin to understand our problems lie in the center of our mind – in need of a Spiritual Psychic change. If you find yourself getting stuck in this area, pray for the courage to continue, and ask for spiritual support.

This is where we discover the exact nature of our wrongs. Addressing each resentment by answering these questions, we are able to see how our self-esteem, personal relationships, sex relations, ambitions, security and/or beliefs were threatened or interfered with. And we are able to see the beliefs from each situation or resentment that became the basis for our justified actions or reactions.

A pattern of beliefs and old ideas will begin to unfold.

An honest examination of self allows the light of the Spirit to heal our lives and free us from the internal prison of our soul.

PRINCIPLE

Rigorous Honesty, Willingness and Trust

STEP FOUR RESENTMENT INVENTORY
Part One - Section One - Column I, II and III

I	II	III
The List: I'm Resentful towards...	The Cause: What did *they* do or What did *they* fail to do...	"Why am I angry?": Hurts, threatens, interferes with my....
- **Person** (individual or group) - **Institution** (government, church) - **Principle** (a belief or attitude)		- **Self – Esteem:** What does this situation tell me about my perception or belief, about who I think I am or who I think I should be? - **Personal Relations :** What does this situation tell me about my perception or belief, about who I think I am or who I think I should be, as well as who I think others are or who they should be? - **Sex Relations:** What does this situation tell me about my perception or belief, about who I think men, women are supposed to be or who they should be regarding sex and sexuality? - **Ambitions:** What does this situation tell me about my perception or belief about who I think I am, who I should be or who I want to be? What did I desire, want or hope for in regards to myself, others or my community, culture or family? - **Security:** What does this situation tell me about my perception or belief about who I think I am or who I should be, and who I wanted to be, needed, hoped for or desired? - **Pocketbook:** What does this situation tell me about my perception or belief about who I think I am or who I think I should be, regarding money and my vocation; as a business owner, employee, homemaker, spouse, parent, child, student or volunteer. What did I want, need, hope for or desire?

STEP FOUR RESENTMENT INVENTORY
Part One - Section One - Column I
Example

Column I—The list of names

- Person/thing

1. Mom
2. Dad
3. God
4. Sister
5. Children
6. Disease/alcoholism
7. People at school/work

etc.

- Institution

1. Medical
2. School System
3. Religious organization/church
4. Police
5. Government
6. IRS
7. Insurance Company

etc.

- Principle

1. I am stupid
2. I must be perfect (size, daughter, husband, provider, Christian)
3. I don't deserve happiness/help/etc....
4. I am only wanted for what I can do or give/not for who I am
5. Godly people are not financially successful or wealthy
6. Life is for suffering, not happiness
7. Alcoholics/drug addicts are bad people

etc.

Chapter Four

STEP FOUR RESENTMENT INVENTORY
Part One - Section One - Column II
Example

Column II—The Cause or reason for each resentment. What did "*they*" do or fail to do?

Person - from Column I
1. Mom
    a. slapped me
    b. came to my school drunk
    c. promised to divorce my abusive stepfather
    d. did not pay for my college and paid for my siblings' college
    e. paid more attention to my older sister

2. Dad
    a. abandoned family
    b. lied about coming to see me
    c. forgot my birthday
    d. arrested for drugs and in prison

3. God
    a. made my grandfather die
    b. made me an alcoholic / food addict / sex addict
    c. didn't cure my friend's cancer
    d. made me feel undeserving (of help, love, etc.)

Continue listing the cause or reason for each resentment for each person in Column I.

Institution - from Column I
1. Medical
    a. not treating me like a person
    b. doesn't listen to me / discounts my reality / doctors say it's all in my head
    c. resent the cost of medicine, exclusive nature of treatment (my grandmother could not afford medicine she needed and died)

2. School System
    a. expects perfection
    b. didn't pay attention when I needed help
    c. teachers said I was slow, did not care, ignored my learning difference

3. Religious organization/church
   a. must be perfect
   b. only men have significant spiritual contributions
   c. judgmental and exclusive
   d. said I was going to hell

Continue listing the cause or reason for each resentment for each person in Column I.

Principle - from Column I
1. I am stupid
   a. I don't know how to do math
   b. I did not finish college
   c. Chemistry teacher told me daily I would fail his class

2. I must be perfect (size, daughter, husband, provider, Christian)
   a. commercials on television and in print portray the perfect physical image of a successful and desirable person
   b. a good Christian loves everyone and does not get angry
   c. my family depends on me

3. I don't deserve happiness/help/etc....
   a. the good die young
   b. I was abused sexually
   c. happiness is only for when you go to Heaven, if you get there, not daily living on Earth

Continue listing the cause or reason for each resentment for each person in Column I.

STEP FOUR RESENTMENT INVENTORY
Part One - Section One - Column III
Example

Column III—"Why am I angry?"

Hurts, threatens, and/or interferes with my:

Self – Esteem: What does this situation tell me about my perception or belief, about who I think I am or who I think I should be?

Personal Relations : What does this situation tell me about my perception or belief, about who I think I am or who I think I should be, as well as who I think others are or who they should be?

Sex Relations: What does this situation tell me about my perception or belief, about who I think men, women are supposed to be or who they should be regarding sex and sexuality?

Ambitions: What does this situation tell me about my perception or belief about who I think I am, who I should be or who I want to be? What did I desire, want or hope for in regards to myself, others or my community, culture or family?

Security: What does this situation tell me about my perception or belief about who I think I am or who I should be, and who I wanted to be, needed, hoped for or desired?

Pocketbook: What does this situation tell me about my perception or belief about who I think I am or who I think I should be, regarding money and my vocation; as a business owner, employee, homemaker, spouse, parent, child, student or volunteer. What did I want, need, hope for or desire?

Person - from Column II

1. Mom
    a. slapped me

       self-esteem: hurt me, tells/told me who I am or that I am nobody

       personal relations: tells/told me women are mean and abusive, not to be trusted

       sex relations: not applicable (or made me ashamed of my feelings)

       ambition: "I wanted/hoped for a close relationship with my mom."

       security: "I wanted to feel safe and not be physically hurt by my mom"

       pocketbook: not applicable (or refused to support me at college)

    b. came to my school drunk

       self-esteem: "I'm bad or she wouldn't drink"

       personal relations: "women are not to be trusted"

       sex relations: "my boyfriend broke up with me, I am only wanted if I have a perfect family"

       ambition: "I wanted to be proud of my family"

       security: "I needed a sober mom"

       pocketbook: "We did not have the money to buy clothes for school, so I would 'fit in' with peers."

    Continue with all the resentments you listed in Column II for each person.

Institution - from Column II

1. Medical

    a. not treating me like a person

    self esteem: "I don't matter"

    personal relations: "Doctors should care and listen to their patients"

    sex relations: N/A

    ambition: "I hoped for caring medical treatment"

    security: "I needed to matter to my doctor"

    pocketbook: "Spent a lot of money and received no help"

    b. doesn't listen to me / discounts my reality / doctors say it's all in my head

    self-esteem: "I'm crazy"

    personal relations: "Doctors think they know it all and are not to be trusted"

    sex relations: N/A

    ambition: "I should be listened to and believed, I wanted to be healthy"

    security: "I needed to get well"

    pocketbook: "Paid for help that was not received"

Continue with all the resentments you listed in Column II for each institution.

Principle - from Column II

1. I am stupid

    a. I don't know how to do math

    self-esteem: "I'm not capable of learning"

    personal relations: "men are smart, women are stupid"

    sex relations: N/A

    ambition: "I wanted a college degree"

    security: "I needed knowledge and to know I could learn"

    pocketbook: "I have to work ten times harder to prove myself (or to keep my job)"

    b. I did not finish college

    self-esteem: "I'm a failure"

    personal relations: N/A

    sex relations: "I believe I'm only wanted for sex"

    ambition: "I wanted a college degree, I hoped to be proud of myself"

    security: "I needed help to learn and to know that I could learn"

    pocketbook: "I'm underpaid"

Continue with all the resentments you listed in Column II for each principle.

Chapter Four
More Support for Resentment Inventory

Don't give up! *Now is the time for the resentment prayer, praying for those who have hurt you. With this prayer renewed strength and courage will come.*

Keep going, you can do this!

MAKE SURE THAT you rest and eat well during this time. This is not the time or place to get stuck in perfectionism. Call your support person for support and guidance if you begin to feel overwhelmed. This step may take some time if you have never before practiced such a deep self-examination of conscience. It may also take weeks to complete this inventory if you have not written one in a long time. Call your support person if you get stuck. Pray for willingness to keep going if you begin to waver and want to give up or stop this process.

Be kind to yourself and honor your willingness to take this action. Remember that most balanced and well-developed persons practice some form of self-examination—you are not alone. The payoff will be great as you create freedom and room for growth by writing your inventory.

Keep in mind that we all have good and bad character traits. We all do things we are ashamed of at some time in our lives. These things must be submitted to the light of the Spirit for healing to take place. Then, in Column IV, you will see clearly what has kept you from living in harmony with your fellows, freeing you to enjoy a happy and useful life.

This may also be a time you become aware of changes that may be taking place in your life. Some well-meaning friends or family may have been watching you change, they may see feelings being expressed that have been absent for years. They may express concern for your well-being while you are changing. Changes in us can be hard for our loved ones. They know you exactly as you have taught them to know you and they know themselves as they have come to relate to you. Now you are changing. Although the change is good and positive, they may become afraid—uncertain of their place in your life as you become the wonderful, talented, healed and whole spiritual human being you were created to be. Be patient with them; some people will stay and some will leave. Gain support from those who have an investment in your wholeness. God is working in your life for your well-being. Trust the process.

Chapter Four
STEP FOUR RESENTMENT INVENTORY
Part One - Section Two - Column IV and V

📖 *Read* from the bottom of page 66 through page 67 in *Alcoholics Anonymous* and pray, the following prayer, before moving on to Column IV and V.

Prayer

Creator, help me show those who have harmed me the same tolerance, compassion and patience that I would cheerfully grant a sick friend. When I am offended help me to remember they may be suffering and show me how I can be helpful. Grant me the grace to avoid retaliation, silent scorn or arguments, as this may destroy any future chance to be helpful. God, help me keep an attitude of compassion and kindness, towards others, as well as myself, and I pray there will be occasions where I may be helpful to others. Save me from being angry and I pray Thy will be done each day in my life."
(paraphrased from page 67 of *Alcoholics Anonymous*)

Now it is time to move on to Column IV, looking at how I acted upon the beliefs revealed in Column III. How did I live/act out (or not act/behave) in my life having had my self-esteem, personal relations, sex relations, ambitions, security and/or pocketbook threatened, hurt or affected? What did I do? What did I not do? How did I feel?

"...Referring to our list again. Putting out of our minds the wrongs others have done, we resolutely looked for our own mistakes."
(page 67 of *Alcoholics Anonymous*)

Again, remember that this is an inventory to find the things that have blocked us from living in harmony with our Creator and those around us.

You are now ready to complete Column IV and V on the following pages, as you will address each situation previously written in Column II and III.

PRINCIPLE
Rigorous Honesty, Willingness and Trust

STEP FOUR RESENTMENT INVENTORY
Part One - Section Two - Column IV and V

IV	V
My mistakes. Where have *I* been *selfish, dishonest, self-seeking* or *afraid*?	Who was hurt? These are the names to be reviewed by the person hearing my Fifth Step for amends in Step Eight.
- what did *I* do / action taken or not taken as a result of my perceptions / beliefs uncovered in Column III - put a S, D, SS, F by each situation to identify each time *I* was *selfish, dishonest, self-seeking or full of fear*	

STEP FOUR RESENTMENT INVENTORY
Part One - Section One - Column IV and V
Example

Column IV—My mistakes

Where have *I* been *selfish, self-seeking, dishonest or afraid?*

Person/Thing - from Column III

1. Mom
   a. I slapped my own daughter—F
   b. I became an overachiever to prove I am somebody—SS, D, F
   c. I avoided relationships with women—D, F
   d. I tried to earn mom's approval so I kept secrets about my mistakes, and when I needed help, I was alone and trusted no one—S, SS, D, F
   e. I withheld any appreciation or honor towards my mother, she owed me—S, SS, D, F
   f. I tried to control or fix other people's drinking—SS, F
   g. I blamed alcoholics for all my problems—S, D, F
   h. If it's my fault, then I should be able to fix it—D, F
   i. I lied about my family to my partner and friends—D, F

Institution - from Column III

1. Medical
   a. I blamed my ill health on doctors and assassinated their characters—D, F
   b. I didn't take care of my health, I smoked and ate unhealthy food—S, F
   c. I stopped paying for insurance—F
   d. I became disabled and lost my job—F

Principles - from Column III

1. I am stupid
   a. I quit college—D, F
   b. I encouraged my son educationally, not my daughter—D, F
   c. I overworked to prove myself and neglected my family—S, SS, D, F
   d. I verbally abuse myself and allow others to put me down—D, F
   e. I'm always late, set myself up to get fired by lying and making excuses—S, D, F
   f. I pretend to be stupid and have few sexual boundaries—D, F

Column V—Who was hurt? Names to be reviewed by the person hearing my Fifth Step.
Amends list

a. My daughter
b. Myself
c. All women as a population
d. Mom
e. Alcoholics
f. Partner and friends
g. Doctor whose character I assassinated.
h. My children and family
i. My employer

Chapter Four
Support for Fear Inventory

THIS IS AN *EXCITING* part of Step Four. I experienced an internal shift—from feeling as if I was full of fear to a sense of freedom from fears that had, at one time, held me captive. You too may experience a similar freedom from fear. It does not matter how silly or how serious a fear may seem, list your fears and answer the questions, to the best of your ability.

Pause when asked to pray, "What would God have me be?".

Let God inspire you. Answers may be very simple—do not complicate this step. Sometimes we are so comfortable living with our fears that we are afraid to be free of them. What would happen? If fear is not my motivator then what is? Is it possible that I could become a person whose motivations are derived from love instead of fear? Am I willing to let go of my fears that are ruling my life and allowing love to take hold?

You may ask yourself, "Would self-reliance stop or change what I am afraid of?" Do not let anything keep you from this part of this process. You deserve to be free from fear. Memorize short phrases that help to vanquish your fears and read them each day for 30 days. This will help you to remember the solution to fear revealed in this part of your writing. Breathing exercises combined with repeating a mantra, helps a great deal. *Trust infinite God*—not in finite self—this became my mantra for years, when dealing with fear, recalling that God is within; not separate from my being, but within me each moment of everyday.

Examples of Fear are: fear of drinking again, fear of having sex or of never having sex, fear of not having money, of being dependent, of having no purpose, of being embarrassed; fear of authority (parents, police or employer), fear of taking exams, fear of rejection, fear of abandonment, fear of people and relationships, fear of failure or success, fear of not having enough (money, support, consideration, etc.), fear of change, fear of accepting things as they are, fear of being responsible, fear of insanity, fear of love or not being loved, fear of being honest, fear of divorce, fear of one's boss, fear of going to jail, fear of flying in an airplane, fear of heights; fear of emotional pain, fear of being separated from one's children, fear of other cultures and races, fear of never getting married, fear of Hell, fear of losing one's parents, fear of letting down those who depend on us, fear of being raped or being raped again, fear of being happy, fear of material wealth, fear of dying, fear of one's family member dying, etc.

Chapter Four
STEP FOUR FEAR INVENTORY
Part Two - Section One - List of Fears

"We reviewed our fears thoroughly."
(page 68 in *Alcoholics Anonymous*)

📖 **Read** from the last paragraph on page 67 through page 68 in *Alcoholics Anonymous.*

✍ **Write a list of your fears. Start with the first fear that comes to mind and continue until all of your fears are listed.**

This is your inventory; do not discount the significance of each fear that comes to mind, no matter how big or small.

✍ **In the second column, ask yourself, "Why am I afraid?" and write those ideas that come to mind. You may not be able to identify a specific reason for each fear, as sometimes we have fears with no known idea of its source and then sometimes we have fears that are inter-generational.**

✍ **In the third column, ask yourself, "Has self-reliance failed?" answer yes or no for each fear. Or ask yourself, "Would self-reliance stop or change what I am afraid of?"**

No explanations are needed or necessary!

Faith is carved out with many experiences, tears, fears and the decision to trust God
– one day at a time –

PRINCIPLE
Rigorous Honesty, Willingness and Trust

STEP FOUR FEAR INVENTORY
Part Two - Section One - List of Fears
Example

My fears are	Why am I afraid?	Has self-reliance failed?
1. Being a failure as a parent	I slapped my daughter	Y
2. Afraid of intimacy with friends	Friends will make fun of you	Y
3. Afraid of taking exams	Always freeze at test time	Y
4. Afraid of heights	I don't know	Y
5. Afraid my parents will die	Dad is sick	Y
6. Afraid my child/children will die	I can't protect them 24 hours a day	Y
7. Afraid of getting fired from my job	I'm always late	Y
8. Fear of never getting married	I'm too old	Y
9. Afraid of going to Hell	I was told I would if I wasn't good	Y
10. Afraid there is no life after death	No one knows for sure, no hard proof	Y
11. Afraid of having sex	My girlfriend got pregnant and had an abortion	Y
12. Afraid of going crazy	There are times I feel like I'm crazy	Y

STEP FOUR FEAR INVENTORY
Part Two - Section One - List of Fears

My fears are	Why am I afraid?	Has self-reliance failed?
1.		
2.		
3.		
4.		
5.		
6.		
7.		
8.		
9.		
10.		
11.		
12.		

Chapter Four

STEP FOUR FEAR INVENTORY
Part Two - Section Two - Solution to Fears
Example

📖   ***Read*** page 68 in *Alcoholics Anonymous* and pray as follows:

"God remove my fears and direct my attention to what you would have me be."

Trusting God, allow faith and inspiration to guide you, as you build a strong foundation, leaving fear behind in the hands and power of God.

✍   **Write a sentence for each fear previously listed asking yourself, "What would God have me be?"***

* *Save this page for review after all of the steps have been completed.*

God would have me...

1. Ask for guidance to learn how to be the kind of parent I want to be.

2. Trust kind, loving friends and to be a kind, loving friend.

3. Disciplined in study preparation and learn new test-taking skills.

4. Trust divine control of my life.

5. Accept the cycle of life and that I will be okay no matter what.

6. Accept my limitations as a parent and trust my abilities to protect and provide for my children.

7. Practice the discipline of getting to work on time and being a reliable employee, remembering that God is my true employer.

8. Trust in divine timing, remembering that in God all things are possible.

9. Trust in the sufficiency of divine grace, and that I am loved as God's creation.

10. God would have me see evidence of the cycle of life within divine creation.

11. Live in harmony, embracing my sexuality and trusting the guidance of my Creator in my sex conduct.

12. Trust in my mental and emotional restoration.

STEP FOUR FEAR INVENTORY
Part Two - Section Two - Solution to Fears

📖   **Read** page 68 in *Alcoholics Anonymous* and pray as follows:

"God remove my fears and direct my attention to what you would have me be."

Trusting God, allow faith and inspiration to guide you, as you build a strong foundation, leaving fear behind in the hands and power of God.

✍   **Write a sentence for each fear previously listed asking yourself, "What would God have me be?"***

❋ Save this page for review after all of the steps have been completed.

God would have me...

1. _____

2. _____

3. _____

4. _____

5. _____

6. _____

7. _____

8. _____

9. _____

10. _____

11. _____

12. _____

Chapter Four
Support for Sex Inventory

THE SEX INVENTORY is an honest look at our sex conduct and beliefs. This is not a list of sexual activity, unless it has been harmful to others or ourselves. This is also a look at how others, and other situations or beliefs, have adversely affected our sexuality or sex lives.

It was suggested that I include a part one for the sex inventory asking first how others have harmed me. Considering my own history of writing sex inventories I was able to see clearly that when I had been given the chance to "have my say" about what "they" did to me first I was able to be completely honest. It seems as though the ego just has to have its say first. When this had taken place, however, I found it was much easier to look at my own conduct around sex and my own sexuality. Over the years of practicing this self-examination, I have never found just the right place to put how and what others did or did not do that affected my sexuality. In some cases I could associate no mistake of mine with the behavior of others, especially in considering my sexuality as a child. Yet I had lied to cover up the experience of being abused, and kept this a secret until adulthood. Later in life I had been promiscuous (by my standards) and had taken advantage of others as a result of what I believed about them and about myself. This is the "why" of the first part of the sex inventory. Write down how others harmed you in the sex area or because of sexuality, and include beliefs, hurts, and betrayals. Remember that this is an inventory of what is not working in your life and not the time to judge anyone. Just provide information about what happened. No matter how trivial or how big, if it adversely affected you and you call it to mind, put it on paper. This does not mean that you or anyone else is or is not a bad person. By this time you may be having just such thoughts or feelings. For some this may be the first time some things have been revealed and feelings of guilt or betrayal may arise. These feelings will pass. The point of the process is to find out what needs to be revealed-what needs to be taken to the light of Spirit to be healed.

The next thing is to be completely honest and look at how we may have harmed others in this area. I avoided answering questions about my sex conduct for the first several years I was using the twelve steps in my life, saying, "there are too many questions to ask myself." I was unable to answer with complete honesty until I was able to tell first how I had been harmed in this area. I also had the false notion that the sex inventory was about intercourse. It is not. It is a good look at this area of my sexual conduct and sexual makeup-nothing more. Sex is another area where many secrets hide and disguise themselves. It is an area where many of us fall short of living up to our ideals and are consequently dishonest.

This dishonesty is based in fear, and fear is a lie. It is not so easy to face the facts of our past sex conduct and how we have harmed others with our attitudes and inconsiderate behavior; still, it is necessary that we do so in order to bring about a new vision for our future sex life/sexuality, ideas and attitudes. The hope and promise of this part of the sex inventory, is to receive divine grace and awaken to the Power of God within you that will help you live in harmony with a new idea of your sex life and sexuality.

I can assure you of one thing: God has healed this area of my life and restored me to a set of beliefs and values that I love and can live with happily. There is nothing our Creator cannot do. Years of healing in this area have made the words *sacred sex* meaningful, which for many in today's culture might be an oxymoron. I have found that my spirituality and my sexuality can be in harmony with one another and not confused, in spite of the subtle or complex ways they are connected.

When you mind map your vision for your future sex life/idea of sexuality allow Spirit to inspire you and create in you a new idea or recover your good, but old ideas—keeping in mind that our sex powers are God-given and good.

Chapter Four
STEP FOUR SEX INVENTORY
Part Three - Section One - What Did *They* Do?

📖 *Read* pages 68-71 of *Alcoholics Anonymous*, paying attention to the second paragraph on page 69. This writing should be continued in your Fourth Step notebook.

✍ *List each person, institution, thing or situation that has adversely affected <u>you</u> in the area of sexuality.*

✍ *Referring to your list, ask yourself, "Where have they been selfish, dishonest, and inconsiderate?" and describe how this occurred. Who was hurt? Did they arouse jealousy, suspicion or bitterness? Describe how this occurred, giving more than a yes or no answer.*

✍ *Write down your sound, sane or reasonable idea of what they could have done instead.*

PRINCIPLE

Rigorous Honesty, Willingness and Trust

STEP FOUR SEX INVENTORY
Part Three - Section One - What Did *They* Do?
Example

List	Where have *they* been:		
	Selfish	Dishonest	Inconsiderate
PERSON (or institution) 1. Grandmother	NA	Told me I would grow up to be a prostitute because she saw me masturbate.	Told me she found me fondling/rocking myself at age 7
2. Dad	Sexually abused me when I was ten	Told me it was my fault	Used me
SITUATION (or incident) 1. Husband had affair with another woman	By thinking only of himself and making the decision to have an affair, broke our marriage commitment	Lied about it when confronted	He told me suspicions were all in my head. Did not consider how this would affect me, our family and our marriage
THING (belief or old idea) 1. Don't ask questions about sex or physical development - no honest communication from adults	No time or trust to teach healthy human sexual development or give information and ideas about sex, protection from STD's and pregnancy.	There was no honest information taught about sex, birth control, STD protection. Adults do not want to see teenagers sexuality.	Didn't consider how lack of honest information affected my behavior with others. Put me at risk for sexual dysfunction, lying, pregnancy and STD's.

STEP FOUR SEX INVENTORY
Part Three - Section One - What Did *They* Do?
Example

Who was hurt?	Did *they* arouse in me or my life...		
	Jealousy	Suspicion	Bitterness
PERSON (or institution) 1. Me	NA	I was afraid of being caught masturbating	I hated her for telling others and humiliating me
2. Me, my mom, my siblings	I was jealous of girls who had normal loving fathers, who treated them as daughters and not as sex objects	I did not trust men sexually or physically; I did not trust women; no one protected me	I hated myself; I believed it was my fault; I hated my mother for not protecting me
SITUATION (or incident) 1. Me	I was jealous and felt inadequate sexually as a wife and believed he would not have had an affair if it was not my fault	Neighbors told me they were together when I was out of town	I blamed myself and became bitter toward him
THING (belief or old idea) 1. Me, sex partners and personal relationships	I was jealous of others who were comfortable and confident with their own sexuality	I trusted no one and was afraid others would find out how little I knew about sex	Bitter towards the opposite sex because I had to perform or be found out. Exposed to STD's and unplanned pregnancy

STEP FOUR SEX INVENTORY
Part Three - Section One - What Did *They* Do?
Example

How were *they* at fault?	What could *they* have done differently?
PERSON (or institution) 1. Grandmother was shaming me about my body and for talking to family openly about my sexuality. I was a child.	She should have told me it was okay and normal for children to touch themselves and discover their bodies and to do so in privacy. She should not have discussed this situation with others.
2. Dad was totally responsible for being sexual towards me and making me a sex object, thus I was confused about proper roles and relations.	He should not have been sexual with me, treated me like a child, not a spouse or a sex object
SITUATION (or incident) Violated marriage commitment to fidelity. Did not honor our commitment to be intimate only with each other.	He should not have had an affair; should have talked to someone before acting on impulses or sought marriage counseling to address the marital difficulties or his dissatisfaction. He should have been honest about his sex ideas and values before we were married. He could have admitted and ended his affair and tried to rebuild marriage and feelings of betrayal with professional counseling.
THING (belief or old idea) The belief kept me from maturing sexually and honoring my sexuality. I was vulnerable to pregnancy and STD's and sexual dysfunction and confusion.	Accurate information about sex/sexuality, physical development, procreation and STD prevention should be available. Value clarification should have been available to help me uncover my sexual values and to allow me to choose my behavior.

Chapter Four

STEP FOUR SEX INVENTORY
Part Three - Section One - What Did *They* Do?

List	Where have *they* been:		
	Selfish	Dishonest	Inconsiderate
PERSON (or institution)			
SITUATION (or incident)			
THING (belief or old idea)			

STEP FOUR SEX INVENTORY
Part Three - Section One - What Did *They* Do? (continued)

Who was hurt?	Did *they* arouse in me or my life...		
	Jealousy	Suspicion	Bitterness
PERSON (or institution)			
SITUATION (or incident)			
THING (belief or old idea)			

STEP FOUR SEX INVENTORY
Part Three - Section One - What Did *They* Do? (continued)

How were *they* at fault?	What could *they* have done differently?
PERSON (or institution)	
SITUATION (or incident)	
THING (belief or old idea)	

Chapter Four
STEP FOUR SEX INVENTORY
Part Three - Section Two - What Did *I* Do?

📖 ***Read*** pages 68-71 of *Alcoholics Anonymous*, paying attention to the second paragraph on page 69. This writing should continue in your Fourth Step notebook.

Now, setting aside how others have harmed you, ask yourself these questions - looking at how you have misused your sex power. Remembering this is a <u>review</u> of our sex conduct, not a time to pass judgment.

✎ ***Writing in your notebook, list persons, institutions, things or situations where you adversely affected another in the area of sexuality.***

✎ ***Referring to your list, ask yourself with each person or situation, "Where you have been selfish, dishonest or inconsiderate?" and describe what occurred. Who was hurt? Did you arouse jealousy, suspicion or bitterness? Describe how this occurred giving more than a yes or no answer.***

✎ ***Write a reasonable idea of where you were at fault and what you could have done instead.***

* This is information of what areas of your sexuality and/or sex life is in need of healing and restoration. This is not a judgment of character; it is an inventory. Leave behind any need to feel shame, judgment or condemnation and, if needed, pray for the willingness to leave these behind.

PRINCIPLE

Rigorous Honesty, Willingness and Trust

STEP FOUR SEX INVENTORY
Part Three - Section Two - What Did *I* Do?
Example

List	Where has *my* conduct been:		
	Selfish	Dishonest	Inconsiderate
PERSON (or institution) 1. Girl in high school	Gossiped about sexually active girl and called her names like "whore" during school as though I were better than she.	I was sexually active and kept this a secret and lied when asked. I promoted myself as a virgin and at church was also dishonest about my sex conduct.	Hurt her with my words and did not consider how this would affect her. I judged her and denied my own behavior.
SITUATION (or incident) 1. I had unprotected sex with various partners and I became pregnant and was ex-posed and exposed others to STD's.	1. I was concerned with myself and having sex. I gave little thought to possible consequences of my actions. I lied to create opportunities to have sex.	1. Lied to friends about working late and mis-sed special event for a good friend. Used work as a way to initiate sex with co-workers which was against company policy.	1. Acted as though I did not care about consequences of sex outside marriage or unprotected sex; did not consider sexually transmitted disease; thought only of my personal gratification; avoided committed relationships.
2. Aborted baby out of fear. Sought no counsel from friends or family. An abor-tion was against my beliefs and desires. Changed mind prior to abortion, but it proceeded and med-ical personnel ignored my plea to stop. I felt raped by the doctor as my "No" was ignored.	2. I did not seek coun-sel from trusted family or friends. I was afraid of losing my job if I was an unmarried pregnant woman.	2. Lied to family and friends when I mis-sed work due to abortion. One friend offered support when she thought I could be pregnant and I lied to her, saying I was not.	2. I gave no thought to the unborn child I was carrying until it was too late. (continued next page)

STEP FOUR SEX INVENTORY
Part Three - Section Two - What Did *I* Do?
Example (continued)

List	Where has *my* conduct been:		
	Selfish	Dishonest	Inconsiderate
THING (belief or old idea) 1. I am inadequate sexually.	1. I was unavailable as a sex partner to my spouse.	1. I made excuses to not have sex.	1. I refused to seek professional help for my sexual dysfunction and ignored my spouse's feelings.
2. I have little value except as a sex partner—that is all I am really good for and no one would want me for who I am.	2. I was inappropriate and brought sexual topics into every discussion or social situation regardless of who was present.	2. Kept number of my sex partners a secret; had sex with people in secret.	2. Ignored other people's discomfort when I would sexualize things during conversations.

STEP FOUR SEX INVENTORY
Part Three - Section Two - What Did *I* Do?
Example (continued)

Who was hurt?	Did *I* unjustifiably arouse...		
	Jealousy	Suspicion	Bitterness
PERSON (or institution) 1. Girl in high school	She lost girlfriends and was treated like an outcast.	Others did not trust me with their secrets.	She was bitter and I shamed her publicly.
SITUATION (or incident) 2. Best friend, employer, aborted child, self	2. Missed best friend's birthday to seek a one time sex liasion.	2. Lied to boss about why I was absent from work. Lied to those who wanted to help and support me through pregnancy.	2. I blamed myself and was unforgiving for the pregnancy and abortion. I was bitter toward the medical profession for ignoring my plea to stop the abortion and I later treated other medical personnel with little respect. Most bitterness was within my soul. I had always wanted a baby and never wanted an abortion. I blamed myself and stayed away from church to punish myself. Felt shamed for judging women who had abortions, having had one. (continued next page)

STEP FOUR SEX INVENTORY
Part Three - Section Two - What Did *I* Do?
Example (continued)

Who was hurt?	Did *I* unjustifiably arouse...		
	Jealousy	Suspicion	Bitterness
THING (belief or old idea) 1. I am inadequate sexually. I have little value except as sex partner - that is all I am really good for and no one would want me for who I am, only for how I can please a sex partner. 2. I flirt regardless of others	1. I am unavailable to my partner sexually. I take no action to initiate a sexual relationship. I take no responsibility for my role. I turn to work to avoid a sex life. 2. Other men/women	1. Partner became suspicious of a possible affair because of my overworking. 2. I was not trusted	1. I took no responsibility for my part and blamed my partner. 2. Other men/women

STEP FOUR SEX INVENTORY
Part Three - Section Two - What Did *I* Do?
Example

Where was *I* at fault?	What could *I* have done differently?
PERSON (or institution) 1. I assassinated the character of a girl at school. I violated confidences shared with me. I was judgmental and a liar about my own sexual conduct.	Been honest with someone about my sexual behavior. Kept my mouth shut about others' behavior and been a trustworthy friend.
SITUATION (or incident) Lied to my best friend about my reason for missing birthday party. Used co-worker for sex. Was irresponsible by taking no precautions to prevent pregnancy or STD's. Went to abortion clinic and did not seek advice or counsel from responsible family member or my church.	Gone to my friend's birthday party. Sought professional help for violating my sex values; asked for help before I put myself in harmful situations. Used protection from STD's. Sought counsel regarding pregnancy. Asked for help, trusted people who cared, trusted God to help me deal with pregnancy; considered the option of adoption.
THING (belief or old idea) 1. I was dishonest with my partner. I became a workaholic to avoid sex relations. I did not seek professional help. 2. I have little value except as a sex partner—that is all I am really good for and no one would want me for who I am, only for how I can please a sex partner.	1. Shared with my partner the truth about feelings surrounding my sexuality and sought professional help. 2. Sought professional help and asked God to help me change my sex ideas and live up to them.

STEP FOUR SEX INVENTORY
Part Three - Section Two - What Did *I* Do?

List	Where has *my* conduct been:		
	Selfish	Dishonest	Inconsiderate
PERSON (or institution)			
SITUATION (or incident)			
THING (belief or old idea)			

STEP FOUR SEX INVENTORY
Part Three - Section Two - What Did *I* Do? (continued)

Who was hurt?	Did *I* unjustifiably arouse...		
	Jealousy	Suspicion	Bitterness
PERSON (or institution)			
SITUATION (or incident)			
THING (belief or old idea)			

STEP FOUR SEX INVENTORY
Part Three - Section Two - What Did *I* Do? (continued)

Where was *I* at fault?	What could *I* have done differently?
PERSON (or institution)	
SITUATION (or incident)	
THING (belief or old idea)	

Chapter Four
STEP FOUR SEX INVENTORY
Part Three - Section Three - Future Sex Life

Set the Spiritual Direction for Your Sex Life

📖   **Read** pages 69-71 in *Alcoholics Anonymous* and pray as follows:

Thanking God first, for the gift of honesty and willingness given thus far and asking God for needed inspiration as you write your sex vision. Ask God for help molding ideals for your sex life, your sexual conduct and desired beliefs surrounding your sex life and your sexuality.

"We remembered always that our sex powers are God-given and therefore good, neither to be used lightly or selfishly, nor to be despised and loathed."
(page 69 in *Alcoholics Anonymous)*

✎   *Mind map your description and characteristics of a sound ideal for your future sex life and sexuality.* *

✎   *Taking words from this mind map, write your vision statement, "I am... ", as you set the course for your future sex life and sexuality.* *

It may be helpful to use your notes from sections one and two, "What could *they* or *I* have done differently?" from the Sex Inventory, to assist you in writing your ideals for your future sex life and your sexuality.

The following pages offer an example of both a mind map and vision statement regarding sex and sexuality.

* *Save this page for review after all of the steps have been completed.*

Rigorous Honesty, Willingness and Trust

STEP FOUR MIND MAP
Part Three - Section Three - Future Sex Life
Example

Ideal / Vision for Future Sex Life

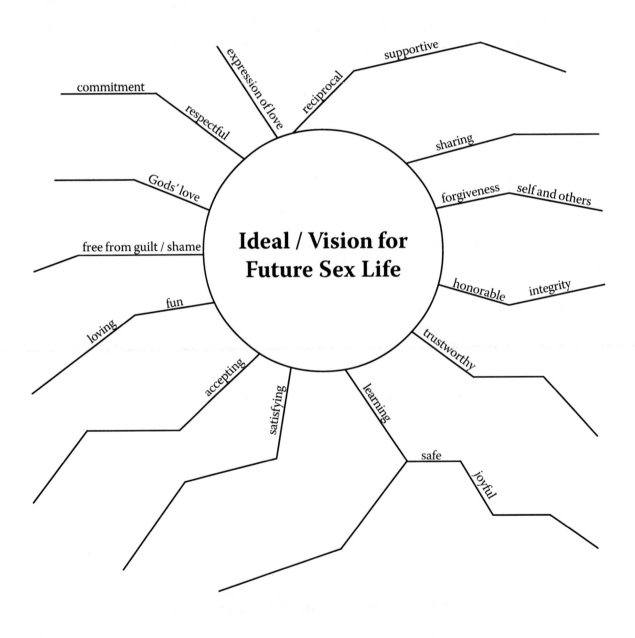

STEP FOUR VISION STATEMENT
Part Three - Section Three - Future Sex Life
Example

Sex Vision Statement

Prayer
Or a similar prayer

God, help me shape a sound and sane ideal for my future sex life as I trust You to guide me in questionable situations. Grant me the strength and grace to do the right thing and help me, with each relation and situation, consider if I am being selfish or not. I trust You to judge my sex situation and whenever I am doubtful, I pray that I will pause, until inspiration and guidance comes.

✍ **Write your vision statement, taking words from your mind map, striving to articulate sane and sound ideals.** *Save this page for review after all of the steps have been completed.*

It may be helpful to review your Step Two and Step Three vision statements as you begin to set forth the vision for your future sex life and sexuality.

"My sexuality is a part of the person I am. I honor and treat myself, along with others with respect, avoiding situations and behavior that would cause me to act in a way that would cause me or any other shame and guilt. I release my old ideas that masturbation is a shameful act or word as I now honor my body and sexuality as I am an expression of a loving Creator.

I honor my new sex life commitments to myself, to others and to God and pray each day for the grace and courage to live as the loving reflection as the woman/man that I was created to be.

I release guilt and shame from the past, and trust God to help me live harmoniously with my new sexuality.

My sex life is a private area of my life, and I avoid pornography and other actions that would cause me shame or guilt.

I dress in a way that reflects the whole human spiritual being that I am created to be, and my dress accurately reflects my values.

I answer honestly, age appropriate questions with my children about sex, pregnancy and sexually transmitted disease, and keep open communication.

STEP FOUR MIND MAP
Part Three - Section Three - Future Sex Life

Ideal / Vision for Future Sex Life

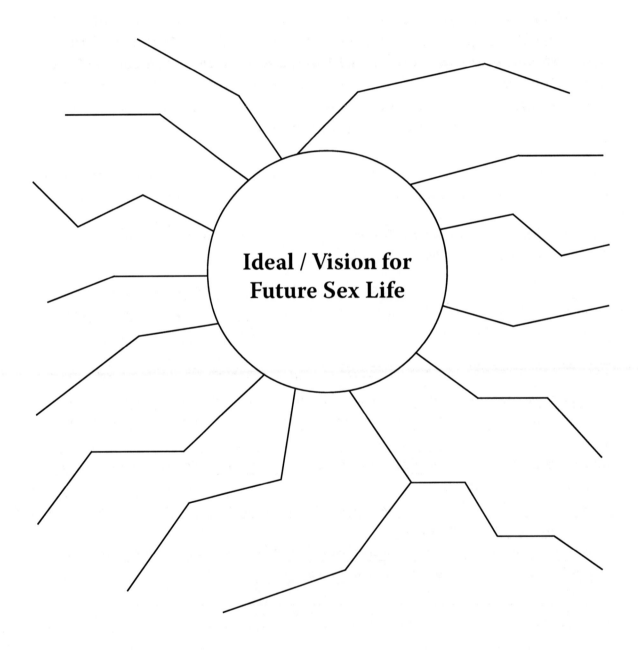

Ideal / Vision for Future Sex Life

STEP FOUR VISION STATEMENT
Part Three - Section Three - Future Sex Life

Sex Vision Statement

Prayer
Or a similar prayer

God, help me shape a sound and sane ideal for my future sex life as I trust You to guide me in questionable situations. Grant me the strength and grace to do the right thing and help me, with each relation and situation, consider if I am being selfish or not. I trust You to judge my sex situation and whenever I am doubtful, I pray that I will pause, until inspiration and guidance comes.

✍ **Write your vision statement, taking words from your mind map, striving to articulate sane and sound ideals.** *Save this page for review after all of the steps have been completed.*

It may be helpful to review your Step Two and Step Three vision statements as you begin to set forth the vision for your future sex life and sexuality.

My sexual ideals / future sex life...

_____
_____
_____
_____
_____
_____
_____
_____
_____
_____
_____
_____
_____
_____
_____
_____
_____

"Repent, then, and turn to God, so that your sins may be wiped out, that times of refreshing may come from the Lord."
Acts 3: 19

Chapter Five
Support for Step Five

TO SHARE OUR WHOLE STORY with another, inviting God to be present, is to experience healing. Read the pages in *Alcoholics Anonymous* that outline *how* the Fifth Step is to be taken and with *whom*. Your story should not be read to a family member. Choose a trusted person who will allow you to read everything you have written, and share the reality of it. This is not the time to prove something or someone right or wrong. Nor is it the time to defend anyone or anything. You are simply admitting those things that have been hidden from the light of the Spirit in order to be set free.

Having shared my Fifth Steps many times, and having heard many Fifth Steps, I can assure you anyone who hears your Fifth Step will be honored to be trusted with such a gift. Ask this person to read pages 72-75 in *Alcoholics Anonymous* so that they will understand the role they are to play in witnessing your Fifth Step. This person may be a member of the clergy, a counselor or a Spiritual Director. Please do not share your Fifth Step with a family member as he or she will have preconceived ideas regarding your emotional well-being and vested interests in the outcome of your self-examination. Things in the inventory which require legal guidance and confidentiality may need to be read to one's attorney.

Plan to spend a number of hours reading everything you've written, going from one page to the next. Ask the person listening to write notes to bring to light your repeated character defects and assets as well as the names of those harmed.

Plan for an hour of quiet afterwards. This may be experienced walking in the woods, sitting by a body of water or in a quiet chapel. This is the time to reflect on your work thus far. If you find you have deliberately omitted something, contact the person hearing your Fifth Step and tell him or her. Do not worry about things that you may have unconsciously withheld, as you will most likely do this work more than once as you recover.

Be prepared to experience the entire Fifth Step, withholding nothing, asking God to help you to be completely honest.

I personally love the power of ritual and find that the symbolic burning of the Fourth Step writings (except for the vision for future sex life and solution to fear) is healing. The flames that devour my history help me to let go of the past. As the flames turn to smoke and rise I can better visualize the way my history has been released to the light of the Spirit.

Experience the courage you have demonstrated so far.

Chapter Five
STEP FIVE

Admit to God, to ourselves, and to another human being the exact nature of our wrongs.

📖   ***Read*** pages 72-75 in *Alcoholics Anonymous.*

Pray for guidance in choosing the person with whom you will take the Fifth Step. Ask the person you have chosen and make a commitment of time sufficient to read the entire Fourth Step.

    "It is important that he be able to keep a confidence; that he fully understand and approve what we are driving at; that he will not try to change our plan. But we must not use this as a mere excuse to postpone." (pages 74-75 in *Alcoholics Anonymous*)

- When you arrive to share your Fourth Step, establish your intention right from the beginning by telling the person listening to your Fifth Step what you are about to do and why you are doing it.
- Next, say a prayer silently or out loud, inviting God to be present as you share honestly with this person your entire inventory. Ask God to guide the person in listening as well.
- Ask the person listening to your inventory to make a list of repeated character defects that have stood in the way of your usefulness to God and others (for Step Six) and assets (for Step Seven). Also, ask him or her to include those you have harmed (persons or institutions), for making amends (Step Eight).
- When you have completed your sharing of the entire Fourth Step, pause and ask yourself if you have consciously withheld anything and if so reveal it at this time. If you have been honest as you could be, thank the person for listening, pause and take a deep breath, acknowledging the courage you have demonstrated.
- Ask for the list of character defects, character assets and the list of amends owed.
- Now would be a good time to burn the entire Fourth Step with your support person, or do so alone during your quiet hour of reflection.

AFTER your Fifth Step, spend a quiet hour and review your work this far as suggested on page 75 in Alcoholics Anonymous.

PRINCIPLE   *Courage and Honesty*

"Whether you turn to the right or to the left, your ears will hear a voice behind you, saying, "This is the way; walk in it"."
Isaiah 30: 21

Chapter Six
Support for Step Six

IT HAS BEEN SAID this is the step that separates the "men from the boys." I prefer seeing this as the step that distinguishes those who are willing to go to any lengths for a life of recovery from those who are not. I have found many times that people (including myself) can be comfortable living with defects of character even when the behavior is making ourselves and others miserable. And family and friends can be comfortable with our defects, even if they are making them miserable—at least they know what misery they can count on and how it will look.

By now you may be getting flack from some people in your life, people who are frustrated because you are not 'acting' like yourself. Some will like the way you are now behaving, living each day willing to have God remove your defects of character, but others will not. Those with whom you have character defects in common—with whom you formerly gossiped, for example—may be the most disappointed. Who or what will you talk about if you change? How will you relate to others? This uncertainty will pass. Things will settle down and some will get used to the more accurate reflection of the real you—and some will not.

The new, more authentic you may make others uncomfortable for a while. Friends and family may wonder where the "old you" went. They may try to resurrect your old behaviors. Be kind and patient with them. We have taught others well as to the behavior they can expect from us. I went through this experience and got through it fairly soon—without some of the people who preferred the "old me."

What would I do if I were happy, useful, and full of unconditional love? Who would take care of me or protect me if I no longer used anger or resentment as a shield of protection? How will I let go and have fun if I am being financially responsible? Who will I blame for any unhappiness in life when I become willing to have my defects of character removed? Growing up is hard at any age. We must let go of defects to develop spiritually. We must trust God and we will be better equipped to deal with life without the familiar shortcomings that we have asked Creator to remove. Some defects may now be in the past while the removal of others will come slowly over a period of time.

Becoming willing to have defects removed that have been standing in the way of my usefulness and happiness is much easier knowing that I am not going to be left as nothing and with nothing. I was afraid that I was mostly made up of defects, and felt protected by them, even though they were the very things that had stood in the way of joyful partnership with God and others in my life. Mind mapping our defects makes it easier to be willing to have God remove them. I found mind mapping what my life would look like without the defect was very powerful and made this step more enjoyable, as I began to imagine myself joyfully anticipating each day without the defect. When I was able to see what I could be like if God removed the defects I was able to imagine having a more desirable character. More humility was required, but at this point

I was becoming comfortable with humility as my companion, instead of something I ran from. Humility was no longer associated with shame or humiliation. Rather, it was a desired asset and the hope of it had been woven into every area of my life.

For now, all that is required is for you to imagine who you would be like or how you would behave if God removed the defects of character that have stood in the way of your usefulness and your enjoyment of living. We so often focus on what is not right in us and in others—this is our chance to see what we are going to be like when we are restored, delivered from our old ideas with our defects of character removed by God. Not only will we have entrusted our character defects and our assets, the "good" and the "bad" to divine care, we will have entrusted the management of our will to God's care as well.

What a relief it was when I finally realized that I no longer needed to struggle with my will—a strong will, at that. The Seventh Step Prayer afforded me the chance to surrender it to God for direction, management and guidance. My will was being managed by the very One who designed and orchestrated the order of life. By Step Seven, then, acting on the idea, the desire and the effort to surrender completely, my will will have become God's.

Examples of defects: jealousy, being dishonest, overly critical, being a perfectionist; sloth; stealing; gossiping or character assassination; being judgmental, blaming; violating sexual commitments, escaping, avoiding commitment; makes excuses, being habitually late, being controlling, justifying, blaming; anger, sarcasm, arrogance (spiritual, intellectual, parental, etc.); hoarding (food, money); lack of respect for money; "you owe me" attitude toward parents, society; being a martyr (won't take needed vacation from work or lunch break, "they need me" attitude), et al.

Chapter Six
STEP SIX

Were entirely ready to have God remove all these defects of character.

📖   ***Read*** the first paragraph, page 76 in *Alcoholics Anonymous*. Reflect on each question and pray for willingness.

✍   **Make a list of the character defects that were revealed to you in Steps Four and Five.**

✍   **Complete a mind map for each defect that has repeatedly stood in the way of your usefulness to God and your fellows.**

Write what you and your life would be like if you did NOT have this defect of character.

Remember that defects previously worked to provide a perceived need, protection, etc. Most of us are unwilling to change or stop hurtful or damaging behavior unless the price of living with these behaviors has become too high. For example, we may feel that there is a payoff in arriving late for work every day as long as there are no adverse results. In short order we may find ourselves arriving late for all our appointments—until the behavior starts to cost us and we perceive our defect for what it is. (Something that is preventing us from leading useful, happy and productive lives!)

PRINCIPLE   *Willingness*

STEP SIX MIND MAP
Example

My Life with God Removing My Character Defects

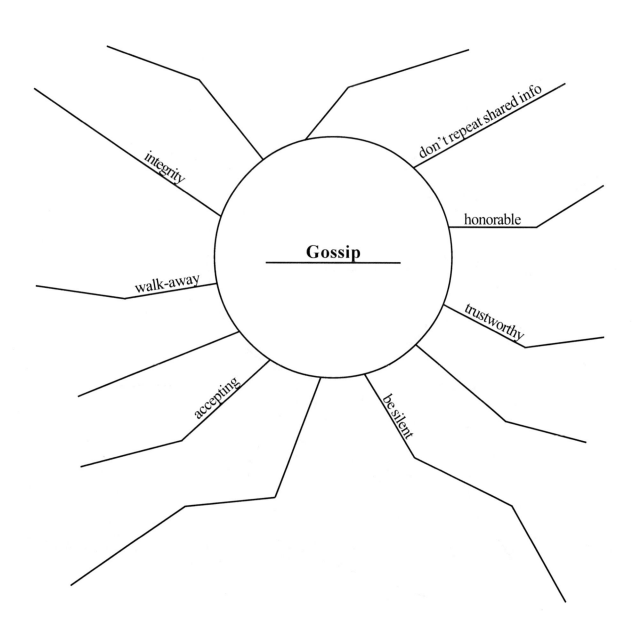

STEP SIX MIND MAP

My Life with God Removing My Character Defects

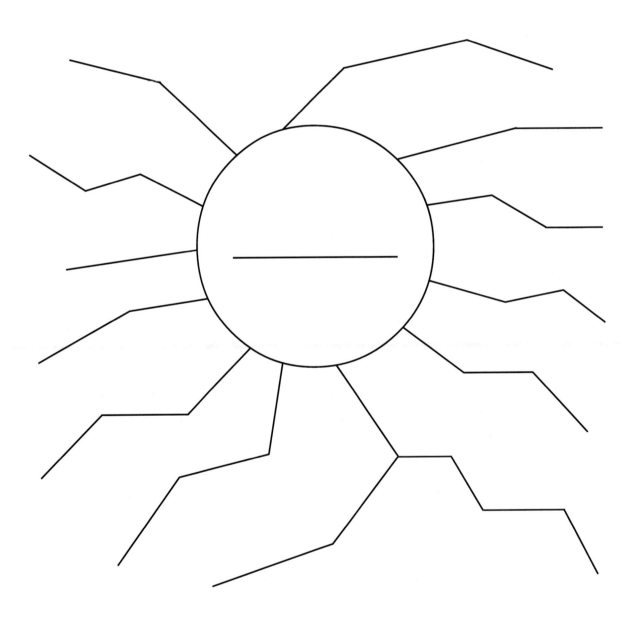

Chapter Six

STEP SIX MIND MAP

My Life with God Removing My Character Defects

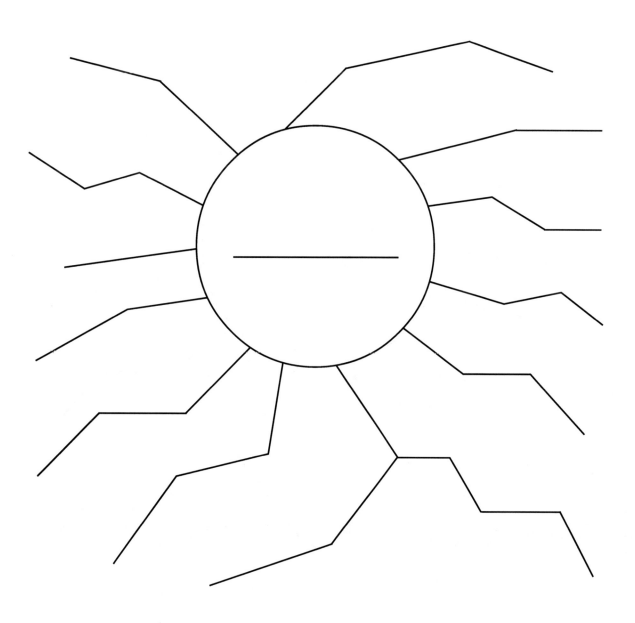

STEP SIX MIND MAP

My Life with God Removing My Character Defects

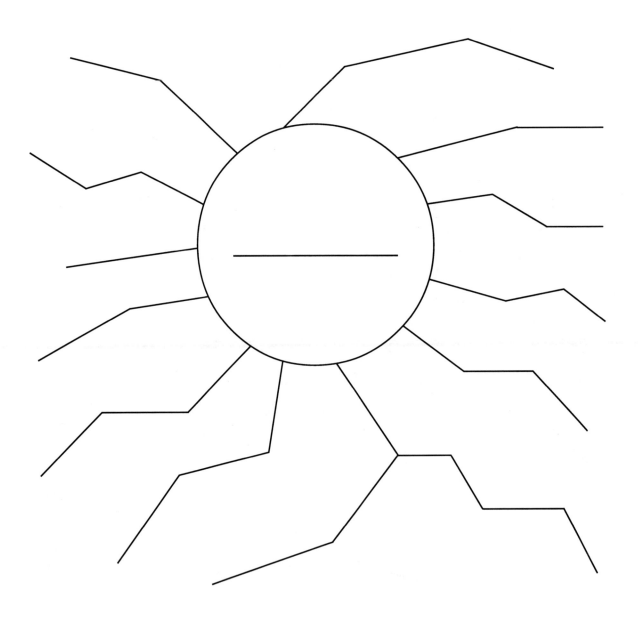

Chapter Six

STEP SIX MIND MAP

My Life with God Removing My Character Defects

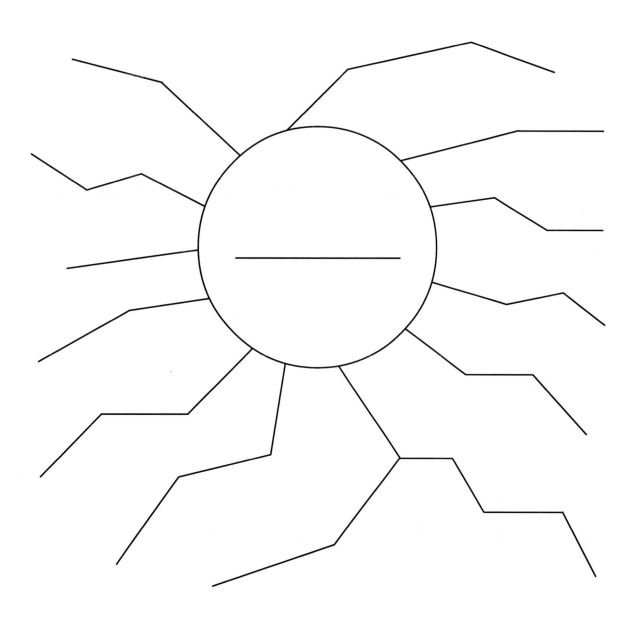

"Therefore, whoever humbles himself like this child is the greatest in the kingdom of Heaven."
Matthew 18: 4

Chapter Seven
Support for Step Seven

STEP SEVEN GIVES US THE CHANCE to go to the Creator as we are, with the good *and* bad. After saying this prayer I first felt what I had imagined it was like to be truly free—free to walk hand in hand with the Creator of the Universe. I was clear about who and what I was offering to my Creator. The good and the bad were out in the open and I trusted in a way I never had before—I was safe and shame was gone.

I had a trusted friend pray with me on bended knee, as I offered myself to God and humbly asked Spirit to remove the defects that had been standing in the way of my usefulness to Him and others. Humility to me is simply being aware of what is, not denying the good or the bad. When I say to myself, *It is what it is,* and *I am who I am,* I'm ready to give myself wholly to God, as is, to do with me as God knows best. Trust was completely alive within me—it was at the core of my being.

I haven't missed the things that were keeping me from fulfilling my purpose. God was big enough to remove the false idea that my character defects would protect me, and relieve me of the bondage to those defects. God was powerful enough to restore me, no matter what! The only effort required of me was to be sincere in my heart. God alone has sufficient power to remove our defects and manage our will. We cannot. God can!

I will never forget the experience of standing before God—with no secrets—nothing hidden, free at last from any need to escape. At last I was able to live in the presence of love, Divine and perfect love.

When I said this prayer I was relieved knowing that my defect of "trying to be perfect" was no longer a needed part of my nature. For the first time I knelt completely naked before my maker and offered myself with complete trust.

Then when I stood up there was an awakening and I knew that from that day forth I would no longer be alone with anything, anywhere, anytime. God and I were one—partners in living. The relationship begun in Step Three was well on its way to a relationship that would work under any and all circumstances. I desired and trusted this relationship and was no longer afraid of being "found out." This was a relationship where I had a place and belonged.

Be available to experience the unconditional love which is possible when you are being totally present *and honest with God.*

Chapter Seven
STEP SEVEN

Humbly asked Him to remove our shortcomings.

📖   ***Read*** the second paragraph on page 76 in *Alcoholics Anonymous*.

✍   ***Mind map your character assets before saying the Seventh Step Prayer.***

✍   ***Make a list of your character assets and defects revealed in Step Five.***

Character Assets	Character Defects
1.	1.
2.	2.
3.	3.
4.	4.
5.	5.

Listing the "good" (assets) and the "bad" (defects) will help to prepare you to honestly and humbly pray the Seventh Step Prayer (page 76). Share with another person the strengths you have listed in the following mind maps and prepare to pray the Seventh Step Prayer (or one with similar principles and ideas). This prayer is suggested to be said with your support person, an understanding friend, family member or Spiritual Director.

This is a vulnerable and special time to go before Creator as you are, with the good and the bad, the positive actions and the missteps. Having no secrets now, we trust God to remove those things which have been determined are those things keeping you from being the person you were created to be.

No one is created bad; this word within the prayer refers to our behaviors that are objectionable, those things which cause and create harm for ourselves, others and creation, it is not about our human condition or design as a human being.

Seventh Step Prayer

"My Creator, I am now willing that you should have all of me, good and bad. I pray that you now remove from me every single defect of character which stands in the way of my usefulness to you and my fellows. Grant me strength, as I go out from here, to do your bidding. Amen."

Humility

STEP SEVEN MIND MAP
Example

Character Assets (the good in me) that I Will Offer to Creator in the Seventh Step Prayer.

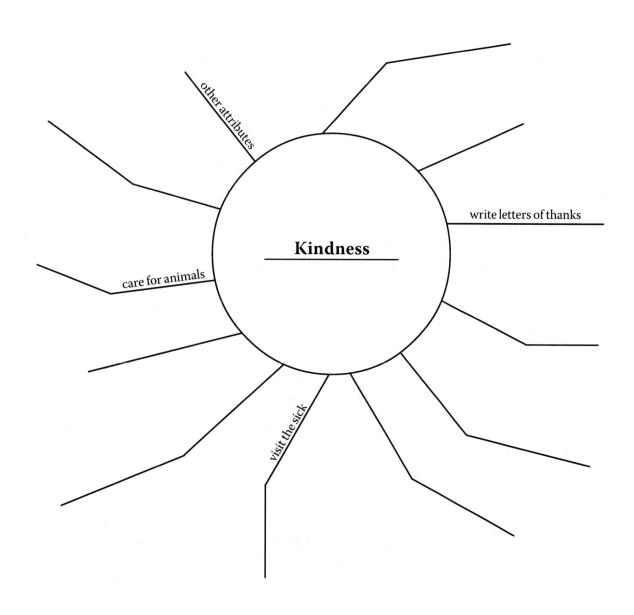

STEP SEVEN MIND MAP

Character Assets (the good in me) that I Will Offer to Creator in the Seventh Step Prayer.
Complete, at a minimum, as many assets as you did character defects.

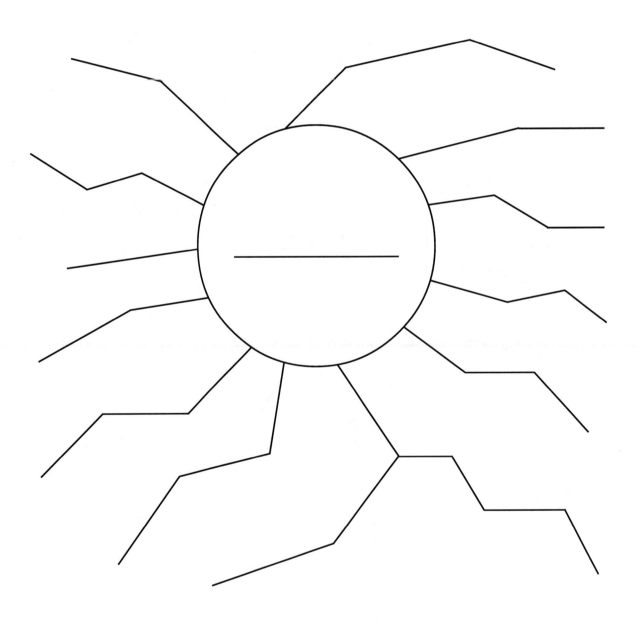

STEP SEVEN MIND MAP

Character Assets (the good in me) that I Will Offer to Creator in the Seventh Step Prayer.
Complete, at a minimum, as many assets as you did character defects.

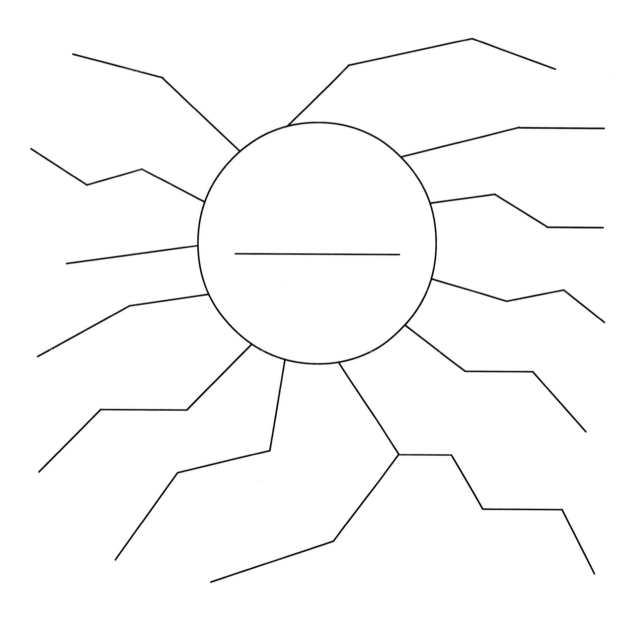

STEP SEVEN MIND MAP

Character Assets (the good in me) that I Will Offer to Creator in the Seventh Step Prayer.
Complete, at a minimum, as many assets as you did character defects.

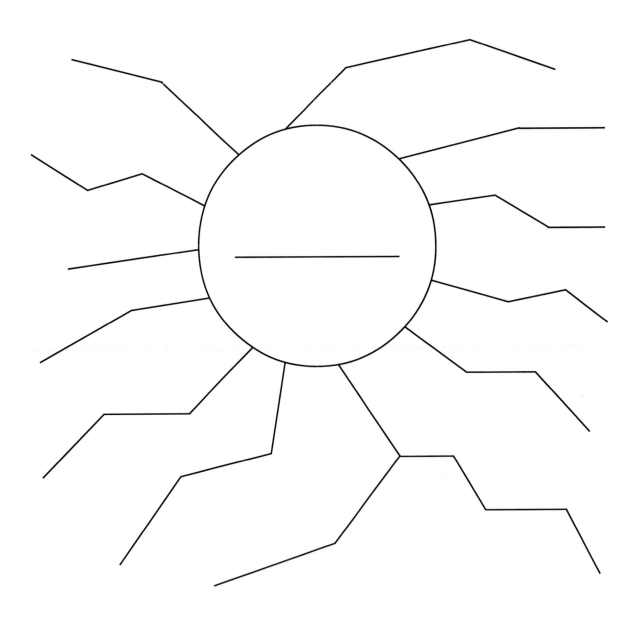

STEP SEVEN MIND MAP

Character Assets (the good in me) that I Will Offer to Creator in the Seventh Step Prayer.

Complete, at a minimum, as many assets as you did character defects.

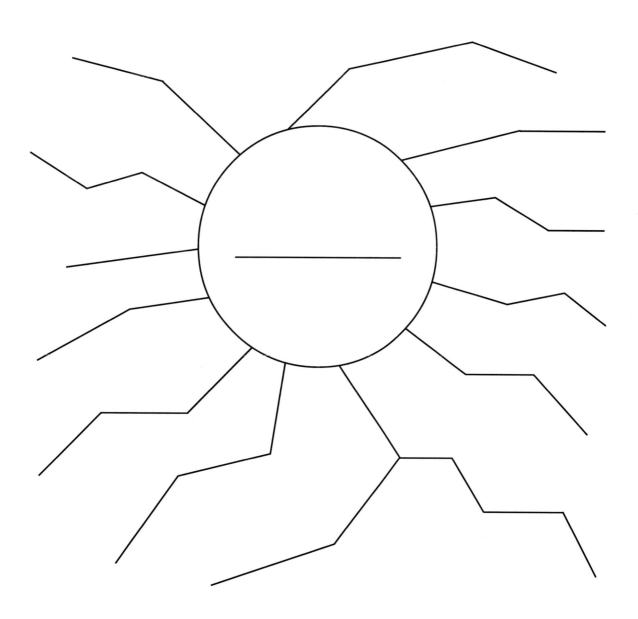

*"For if you forgive men when they sin against you,
your heavenly Father will also forgive you."*
Matthew 6: 14

Chapter Eight
Support for Step Eight

THIS IS THE STEP that allows me to repair any damage and harm caused either by my actions or lack of action. When Step Eight and Step Nine have been completed, I will be able to look the world in the eye without fear of being "found out." I will be free of a life of duality; my actions and beliefs will be in harmony, deeply rooted in my character. No matter how insignificant or how big the messes or mistakes, I will have cleaned them up, though some amends may not have been accepted. No matter, the point is that I will have gone to those I have harmed and told them the truth, and when possible, I will have set right my wrongs. This Eighth Step is about me becoming *willing*, as well as humble, to take the necessary action so that I can live free from the pains, fears, isolation and humiliations of the past. Thus will I find the mental, emotional and spiritual energy to live in the present.

Before we move forward, I would like to share something I learned a long time ago about forgiveness. This is especially important if you were hurt or disappointed in childhood by adults you trusted for your care or well-being, or harmed at any time in your life when you were powerless to defend yourself. Good *can* come from all things, as long as we surrender to God for care, guidance and wisdom. There came a time in my healing process when I simply could not forgive some wrongs that had caused me harm, though I was willing. I was willing to forgive, I had prayed for the power to forgive, still I could not. Yet willingness turned out to be a key ingredient in my forgiveness. About the same time I was struggling with this "how to forgive," I happened to be reading a book about the life of a deeply religious woman, Corrie ten Boom. It was her experience that offered me hope that I could be free from those I had been unable to forgive. Forgiveness had not been found through my own power, nor I could release my heart from the injustices that at times were insurmountable. After I read her experience with forgiveness, I got onto my knees and thanked God for everything that had ever happened to me and for the strength given to me over the years that saw me through those times when I had been deeply injured. This all sounded quite crazy to me, but my spirit encouraged me to do this seemingly simple act. I said the words, "Thank you God for being in my life, and thank You for all of the things that have ever happened to me that have caused me deep pain and suffering, so much that I cannot find it within me to forgive. Jesus, your son asked this same question, as he was innocent when he was murdered and he wanted forgiveness for those who brought him to his death. He asked You to forgive them. Please God forgive those in my life who have harmed me, *forgive them through me* as I cannot. I love You and thank You." Amen.

I rose from the side of my bed and with a resting soul I slept, comforted with my trust in God's power to forgive. With me no more than the channel, through Him I would be free.

That was all it took to allow me to move forward with the injustices of life, no longer needing to understand, accepting that God had a plan for my life and that my concern should be to live my life guided by principles.

Your letters of amends may be written to any person or institution or thing, existing or past, living or dead. If, after discussion with your spiritual advisor, you believe that making direct amends will bring more harm to others, it may be decided that it is best to leave some people alone and stay away. This could be a time to make amends with a bit of creativity. If you would harm a former friend, one whom you have stolen money or goods from, then a letter and the money owed could be the best way to make amends. If gossip is part of your relationship, a direct amends may help you to correct this character defect. One can write a letter admitting the truth in all situations, but guidance will help you choose whether to make a direct amends by letter or by another means.

In relationships there is usually a bit of blaming and defending going on. The letter you write should be focused on what you have done or failed to do, letting the recipient of your amends know that your behavior is not caused by another! This is the time and place to pray and ask for the courage to speak the truth about our shortcomings to those who have been harmed by our action and/or inaction. Simply writing the truth about your action in a letter is a powerful tool that will open wider the door of your soul to bring forth the necessary courage and willingness for Step Nine. Writing these letters is not easy. To stop the blaming and take the necessary action to clean up your "side of the street" is something no one but you can do, with the aide of your Higher Power. And this is the path that will allow the releasing of long-held guilt. Simply saying "I'm sorry" and "letting it go" is insufficient. Humility with honesty is required and not negotiable.

Your letter is to include what you have done to harm the person in question and the motivation behind your action (fear, jealousy, lack of consideration). It is to include your *former* ill feelings, your defects of character and the nature of your wrong. An example of this may be as simple as admitting to another how you blamed and judged him or her out of your own fear of failure, or as an example of dishonesty, how you smiled and behaved as though you agreed with something that you actually opposed, in order to avoid conflict. I found that I needed to include myself in making amends along with those I had hurt—I had treated myself with harsh judgments and withheld gentleness from myself as much as I had harmed others. A letter of amends to one's self, read to your spiritual advisor, can be very healing. I also needed to include God for the times I hurt His children, blaming Him for things people did and for the times my behavior and/or language was a misrepresentation of Divine Love.

By now you get the idea: amends are for anyone I harmed. My wrongs to others are about *me* not them! Continue to pray for those who still cause you difficulty—through gritted teeth if necessary. Pray for their health, their happiness and their good, and don't waste time questioning your sincerity while you do so.

At this step I have seen people promote themselves at times as being worse than they were and more of a bad person than the truth would indicate. I was such a person! We weren't trying to fool anybody, we were just looking for things we had done wrong. In spite of our zeal, our humility wasn't real and it wasn't healing. Making amends in such a way is not telling the truth, it supports being a victim to the disease, without the aid of an Omnipotent and loving God. The truth may well be that we're not so good at being bad. Sometimes we need to make amends to ourselves for the times we have hidden our goodness or wonderful talents as fear took hold, believing a bad-guy, no-good persona was more deserving of attention than that of a kind and gentle, talented person. Fear of vulnerability keeps love hidden and protected, and while we are ruled by our fear we will see our soul's goodness die a little bit each day. A letter of amends to ourselves, written with honesty, love and kindness, wherein we see ourselves as a wonderful creation of the Creator of all life, can heal by releasing the burden of self-hatred from our lives.

People will sometimes make amends for really tough things like murder or stealing and then avoid making direct amends for things like blaming, gossiping, lying, judging, or harboring ill feelings. These cannot be excluded, although one may justify such an exclusion with the idea that one is preventing further harm. The only person we go easy on is the other person, not ourselves. It takes humility to take this step, and to gain enough humility, we simply need to ask our Higher Power for it. Without making direct amends all the work you have done so far will eventually crumble. It could happen a little at a time or all at once, but it will crumble without these amends. The letters are an important tool to keep the focus of amends off of the other person and squarely on you. I have seen many people stop at this point, saying they don't want to hurt the other person, or that they want to wait for the right time. Sometimes this makes perfect sense, but often it does not, and what is at issue is mere fear and a lack of willingness to be thorough.

Writing the truth about my action, such as the time I blamed others for my fears and the times I participated or initiated gossip due to my own jealousy, stopped the insanity of dishonesty and helped restore my character. This was another step where "old ideas" found their way into my consciousness. Again, all that was required was God's grace and power. But again, too, without humility, the wonder of life that gives your eyes that newfound twinkle will *eventually* begin to fall apart if you haven't made all of your direct amends. Amends are not an option. Writing the letters, supplies needed humility, courage and willingness, and helps you to be very clear about what you are making amends for, keeping the focus on you, not others.

Read your amends letters to your spiritual director before making any amends and ask for guidance in making any necessary changes. After making any changes and deciding how to make the amends, read your letters again. Then make plans and commitments to make the amends.

Another word of support for amends. This step says we become *willing to* make amends to those we have harmed. Writing letters to each person, place or thing is a tool that helps humility and willingness to come about. We can only make amends for those things we are aware of. It is impossible to make amends for those times we created harm and knew nothing of it—even with scrupulous evaluation. So, for the harm done to others, unaware and unintentional, do a blanket amends with a letter to all who were harmed. For example, there can be no recall of harm done during a state of alcoholic blackout, though you were actually present. Make amends when you become aware of any harm created by your behavior. We can amend only what we are aware of, no more and no less.

You may also include as worthy of amends the times you withheld the truth about love, respect or appreciation. For example, you might make amends to parents for never telling them of your love or appreciation. Tell the truth always, as long as it will not bring about more harm to others.

For me personally it was very important to include things I had withheld in my amends letters. One example was the honor, appreciation and compassion I withheld from my mother. Never had I told her how important she was to me. I had only told her of my love in sappy greeting cards.

I had held onto my anger over the many mistakes she had made as I was growing up. I had denied her honor, as my elder and for the things she did well. I had denied her compassion for the tremendous difficulty she must have had as a single mother raising and providing for four young children. This was a woman who had worked hard and stayed up late to sew the most beautiful long skirts for her daughters to wear to Church on Christmas morning. There had never been an in-between in my feelings about my mother; condemnation had poisoned all of them. Now, I let go of her mistakes and admitted mine. I was able to see us as two adult women who were mothers, each of whom had made mistakes along the way. Two women, a mother and daughter, who loved each other in their own unique and worthy way.

You may close your letters with a question, asking the person addressed if you have left anything out that you owe an amends for. Also, include in your letter a description of the behavior they can expect from you in the future. And ask them if there is anything further you can do to rectify the harm you have done.

A short story about amends. When I was a young teen, I went to a very large religious gathering for teens, in a distant and large city. I was there out of interest in having fellowship with schoolmates on a trip and my hopes of securing a boyfriend far outweighed my desire for religious education. As a Catholic girl in a small town in East Texas I had no fellows my age to share in my religion—our religion was undesirable and fellows were few and far between. At this gathering, a video was shown professing that when we die and stand before God, everyone we know will stand with us, and all of our deeds would be shown like a movie—broadcast before millions and God. All our secret thoughts and actions would be shown on Judgment Day. Well, by the time I was 16 I had acquired many feelings of shame and had hidden and tucked away many actions in the recesses of my soul, so that on this day of gathering I felt doomed, no matter what.

Years later I went out and made amends to those I had harmed, no matter how small the harm, and I recalled that day in the early '70s. After making my amends, the fear of Judgment Day that had remained with me all those years no longer mattered. I had freely revealed myself to God and others and to myself; thoughts of a fearful Judgment Day were finally gone. God's love, forgiveness and mercy had recovered my soul.

Practicing all of these steps brought me to an acceptance of my shortcomings as well as others'. Having accepted the imperfection of my own human nature I was by now intertwined with God's Grace and love and I began to live as the spiritual human being I was created to be. With God's Holy Spirit as my daily companion, I once again looked forward to living.

One last thought—Keep Going—Don't stop now!

You can do this!

Pray for willingness and courage, it will come.

Chapter Eight
STEP EIGHT

*Made a list of all persons we had harmed and became
willing to make amends to them all.*

📖   **Read** pages 76—84 in *Alcoholics Anonymous.*

✒   **Create a list of who or what is owed amends based on your Fourth and Fifth Steps (this may include individuals, institutions or groups).**

Remember, the list is "all persons we had harmed" not those we are going to see face to face.

✒   **Write an amends letter to each person/institution and share it with someone (sponsor/spiritual director) asking for guidance in questionable situations <u>before</u> making amends.**

Pray before you begin to write, asking God to give you the Grace to write your amends letters with honesty and truth.

> *The letter may include:*
> - *Intention* (to make amends and repair harm done).
> - *The specific wrong committed by you* (blaming, lying, stealing).
> - *The true motive behind the wrong* (fear, jealousy, insecurity, excessive dependency). Avoid any mention of wrongs by others.
> - *What your commitment is for future behavior* (honesty, pay money back; name the behavior to expect).
> - *Asking them, if you have left anything out,* if you have not mentioned any other harm caused that you owe them amends for, and asking if there is anything specific you can do to amend your wrong.
> - *Include a silent or verbal prayer or blessing for the health, happiness and prosperity of those we have harmed.* Remember, we pray for those we resent as they too may be spiritually ill.
> - *Thank the person for seeing you and leave.*

📖   **Read your amends letters and discuss your ideas for creatively making amends to your spiritual director or support person.**

PRINCIPLE

Willingness

"Therefore, if you are offering your gift at the altar and there remember that your brother has something against you, leave your gift there in front of the altar. First go and be reconciled to your brother; then come and offer your gift."
Matthew 5: 23-24

Chapter Nine
Support for Step Nine

BEFORE DECIDING who to make "direct" amends to, discuss the matter with your sponsor or Spiritual Director and in questionable situations, pray. Ask for guidance and inspiration as to how to make amends to those you may not see face to face, i.e. creditors or those who have died or those to whom you might bring further harm. Make the appointments and go make the amends.

I follow a three-time rule. I make three appointments or attempts at making them. First I tell the person what I am doing (making an amends for harm that I have caused). If for reasons out of my control, i.e. they cancel repeatedly, or say this is not a good time, I trust God's wisdom. God knows the perfect time for amends. As long as I am willing to make a direct amends I can trust the timing of the process. The amends may be best made at a later time, or privately with your Spiritual director., with whom it is important to review this step before taking it.

Read your amends letter to the person, institution or place.
Reading the letter keeps the focus on the amends.

Letters can still be read to a person, institution or place or thing that is *not physically present. Speaking your amends is healing and releases you and the other person, even if they have no knowledge of being harmed by you.*

Ask someone to stand in for a person/thing to whom or
to which you are not able to make direct amends.
Have your letter of amends witnessed by a trusted friend.

By this time you will likely be aware of many positive changes within you and your world. Your awakening will have begun. Read your Step Two again and check to see what has already come about. You may find yourself stalling at this step. Please don't. *Amends must be made, even to the spirit of those harmed, or your work will eventually fall apart.* After all of the work thus far you deserve to be free to live in the realm of the Spirit, and to escape the nagging fear of not being thorough. Without this step of direct amends, enough humility will not have been experienced to support a psychic change and your desired spiritual awakening.

Once I had taken this step I no longer feared running into persons I had hurt. I was no longer willing to gossip or participate in character assassination if doing so would cause me to make more amends. Making amends for causing harm is a spiritual discipline that holds us accountable and in the process frees others from the lies we have perpetrated (It is them! *They are at fault!*)

Chapter Nine

After my letters had been read and reviewed, I simply started making appointments and prayed for the willingness to go to each of the people on my list. My mom, my kids and my husband were at the top of the list. I was told to go to it, so I did, and the payoff was big.

When I read the letter to my mom she cried along with me as I told her of the compassion I now had for her and how wrong I was for all the judgments I had made of her as a mother and as a woman. I told her how much I appreciated her and thanked her for caring for us under difficult circumstances. I honored her—maybe for the first time. Our relationship has never been the same. She kept that letter, and a new relationship based on honesty and trust had begun.

I learned something then. Unless I can honor my mother I cannot honor yours, and I will probably not be honored as well. This process has freed me to do just that.

I completed my amends and moved forward with the rest of the process.

Remember: by now we have set aside the wrongs others have done and we are focusing on cleaning up our own messes. We are taking spiritual responsibility and putting it into action. We keep praying for the right time and the willingness to make amends for as long as it takes and all are completed.

Some amends may take years to complete—God/Spirit knows the way and time. Reading my letters also helps me keep the focus on my part—the truth, keeping me from the tempting behavior of justification or blame.

Making direct amends is an action that builds character and trust. This allows us to live mentally and emotionally in the present—to experience the *now* of God and the good of living.

Chapter Nine
STEP NINE

*Made direct amends to such people wherever possible, except
when to do so would injure them or others.*

📖 **Read** pages 76—84 in *Alcoholics Anonymous*.

*"Reminding ourselves that we have decided to go to any lengths to find a
spiritual experience, we ask that we be given strength and direction to do the
right thing, regardless of the personal consequences.* (page 79 in *Alcoholics Anonymous*)

It is also suggested that we secure permission for the amends from all who will be affected.
An example for such an occasion would be if an amends is owed to one's child and another
person/parent was involved in the offense, then that person/parent would be consulted. If consent is not secured then seek the counsel of your spiritual advisor or sponsor.

Make your amends praying for willingness. Go to it!

- Set appointments for those to be seen face to face.
- Go see those persons (traveling if needed) and read your letters, one person at a time.
- Call creditors to make arrangements for financial amends, that you can fulfill.
- Set aside time and create a sacred space to read amends letters to those you may not see face to face. An example would be: Those who have died, institutions, groups of people, the spirit-consciousness of those you can not speak to. You may invite your support person to sit in a sacred space as the representative of those receiving the amends.
- Be creative for amends owed to those not living. Do something in their honor.
- For any children who have died, especially babies aborted or miscarried, or for children given for adoption, babies stillborn or for estranged children—this is a chance to speak your love, grief, or sorrow.
- Plant a rosebush to represent this child, take care of it and nurture it, pulling weeds to protect it, caring for it as you would a child in need of your protection.

*Notice how the promises on pages 83—84 are coming true in your life
as you begin making amends.*

Do not stall or stop five minutes before the miracle!

PRINCIPLE **Courage**

"...for all have sinned and fall short of the glory of God"
Romans 3: 23

Chapter Ten
Support for Step Ten

THIS IS A PRACTICE of discipline that takes effort and a little time each day. However, you will find that this process of self-examination will easily become part of your daily life after awhile.

Discipline is about creating a sense of security and safety. We all need boundaries for our lives and the Tenth Step creates them. One old idea about boundaries and discipline is that it is about control, not safety and security. I can assure you that a child with structure and daily rituals for living is secure in its care. Feeling confident and safe, children with structure will grow into new skills without losing their sense of excitement or wonder.

In the beginning—for those who have not practiced daily self-examination before—reading the suggested questions for a personal inventory each day will help with the practice. I would like to encourage you to continue this practice each day, especially once your life is restored and balanced, as this is one of the steps that helps in the maintenance of our new way of living and the application of these principles. Many spiritual leaders throughout history and across the globe have several practices in common, and self-examination is one of them.

Once this has become part of your daily life, seemingly with little effort you will begin to notice when you are off track in the practice of these principles by means of a twinge of discomfort in a very real and physical sense. Thus it is important for you to pay attention to your "gut," and start listening to that part of you. When my "gut" is in knots or uncomfortable I will check out what is going on within me or around me. This is also considered an early stage in listening, once again, to your intuition. Children know when they are uncomfortable, although they may not have the power of reason to explain their discomfort in a situation, they do listen and voice their sense that something isn't right. Many of us simply forgot to listen to this inner self, this sense of something not being quite right and it is now time to listen again to this feeling of discomfort. Pause and reflect on your actions or thoughts, then check out your surroundings. Perhaps something happened early in the day. In some cases, the gut reaction may come days after a new fear or resentment has cropped up. That is okay, too. Some people are more developed in this area. We are all still able to work this step. No one, unless he or she can not be honest, is incapable of taking time out when their gut gets tight to ask a few simple questions and to evaluate the day so far. Call someone for help; practicing this step is frequently easier if you run it by another person.

I believe most of us have a "sense" when something is going on, good or bad. Many of us have simply disregarded our intuition most of our lives and we no longer rely on it. This is a time to allow that part of us to reassert itself. And for those young enough not to have forgotten this "sense," you may help your older counterpart.

As children some of us were aware of this 6th sense—our intuition or our spirit nature—but discouraged by a lack of guidance or encouragement we set it aside before it could develop. I personally tried to drown out God-consciousness within me and had no idea what to do with intuition or how to discern the guidance of my internal spiritual voice.

With good and trusting guidance, and with the practice of the principles set forth in this workbook, I have come to listen and trust, discern and seek good counsel. I have recovered my intuitive self along this journey, a nice surprise.

Practicing daily inventory is another action that lays a solid foundation for living as you are uncovering or discovering the God-created and inspired use of your spiritual gifts.

It will become easy to clean up new messes (and all of us will make them)—as this is the step that always shows me a way to start a new day—each day—no matter what. This is the open door through which new mistakes will be dealt with and new lessons will be learned. Perfection is not required or desired. All that is needed is a sincere desire and willingness to practice honesty and self-examination, and to continue making any new amends that may become necessary as we go through the day.

This step is truly freeing when you become accustomed to being happy and living free of chaos and misery. Living in harmony and laughter, knowing there will be days of pain and sorrow again will simply be okay, as this step allows me to be the human spirit I was designed to be and to maintain my restored life. Never needing to bury errors through denial, blaming or avoidance helps me to avoid missteps so that I can arrive at an honest appraisal of how I have lived each day. Keeping it very simple, I can end my day with thanks to God for a day well lived. Or when I have taken action that is out of harmony with these principles I share my mistakes with my spiritual director or sponsor. I make amends when needed and ask God to help me do better the next time. Addressed in this manner there is no need to replay our mistakes over and over in our minds.

I found that with time and practice, along with years of effort and encouragement I have grown from an insecure young adult to a confident mature woman. Self-examination has become relatively easy for me today. I can rely on my intuition, seeking wise counsel in questionable situations, I am free to live harmoniously with life. I recognize this is not easy for everyone but I trust it will become so with practice and guidance.

Again, this is a step of discipline. I wrote in my Step Three vision that I desired a relationship with God that would be reciprocal. I desired a relationship where I could trust Him/Her but also a relationship in which I could be trusted and God could count on me. Life has shown this to be the case as opportunities presented over time, some as difficulties, have demonstrated the truth of our deep love and commitment to each other.

I trust God's faithfulness and no longer do I have the insatiable need for proof of being loved by the Creator of life. I hope that God now has trust in my dependence, trust and faithfulness to Him. I am a disciplined spirit today and I have learned to follow good orderly directions, continuing to use common sense, and today my Step Three vision has come about to the extent that God can count on me to be a trusted partner and loyal servant.

God confidence *is a gift of grace open to all and for me this has come as a result of the previous steps and the daily practice of Steps Ten, Eleven and Twelve.*

Chapter Ten
STEP TEN

Continued to take personal inventory and when we were wrong promptly admitted it.

📖   **Read** pages 84—85 in *Alcoholics Anonymous*.

✍   ***Daily inventory: Practice answering these questions each day***
1. Have I been selfish, dishonest, resentful or afraid today?
2. Pray, asking God at once to remove the presence of character defects.
3. Discuss character defect and any harm done with someone immediately.
4. Make amends quickly to those who have been harmed.
5. I then turn my thoughts to someone I can help.

"Love and tolerance of others is our code."
(page 84 in *Alcoholics Anonymous*)

"If we have carefully followed directions, we have begun to sense the flow of His Spirit into us. To some extent we have become God-conscious. We have begun to develop this vital sixth sense. But we must go further and that means more action."
(page 85 in *Alcoholics Anonymous*)

List a variety of ways you are experiencing the flow of Divine Spirit within you and your awareness of your God given sixth sense, your intuition and opportunities now present for good and proper use of your spiritual gifts.
1.
2.
3.
4.
5.

PRINCIPLE   *Discipline*

*"*⁶ *Do not be anxious about anything, but in everything, by prayer and petition, with thanksgiving, present your requests to God."*
*"*⁸ *Finally, brothers, whatever is true, whatever is right, whatever is pure, whatever is lovely, whatever is admirable—if anything is excellent or praiseworthy—think about such things."*
Phillipians 4: 6, 8

Chapter Eleven
Support for Step Eleven

THIS STEP ALSO requires us to practice daily discipline. I began in the late '70s attempting meditation for healing and loved it. It only takes practice and direction from someone experienced, and there are helpful resources today. When I practice, just doing it each day, I find I can begin to *rely* on inspiration and intuition. Intuition is what some call that "gut" feeling or knowing without direct conscious awareness. As I now rely upon this—I have learned; evidence always follows inspiration or intuition. It may take some bit of time but God always follows Spirit's nudging with evidence or coincidences. It is in this way that I am shown to be on the right track, or shown that I need to turn around or to stop. First I practiced listening to inspirations. The more I was willing to trust my practice, the greater my ability to discern God's guidance.

One late afternoon when I was able to go home early from work, I was hoping to grab a quick afternoon nap before my children were home from school, when I felt a sweet nudging to go to my daughter's school. At first my need for a nap seemed more important, as I had been working many hours and was tired—it was a vulnerable time for me, a time when I might be a bit edgy. But this nudging inside of me would not go away, so I drove to my daughter's school, where the students had been dismissed several minutes before I arrived. As I drove into the drive of the school, students were swarming in front and I could see no adults or teachers in sight. I got out of my car to see what trouble was causing this large gathering of students, I suspected someone injured or a fight was brewing and I was correct. My daughter caught sight of me before I found my way into the center of the group of kids and she told me her dear friend was about to be beaten up by another girl. I called out to her friend and told them both to get into my car right away, and with gratitude they did. They were very happy to see me, grateful to have a way out of a fight and curious at the same time why I was there. All I could say was I "felt" that I had to be there. We drove home and I gave myself a quiet time to settle my nerves with a nice period of meditation. This example is only to demonstrate the following of the internal nudging that I believe is a way for God to offer guidance. This intuition that is part of our human makeup can help us to be of use in many ways.

I am certain that you will recall your own experiences of listening to or ignoring God's inspirations. I assure you that as you commit more time each day to your relationship with God you will become more aware of the Divine presence in each day, and God's hand in all things.

For me this has come with practice, with the discipline of daily prayer, with the reading of sacred and holy writings and with meditation. Time to be still and "pause" when agitated or doubtful along with an internal sacred space are my resources until serenity returns. I am able to make much better decisions when my spirit is calm and at peace having time alone with God to be still, to praise with a grateful mind and to listen with my "spiritual ears" for guidance and inspiration. With the practice of meditation I am able to go to the calm within me as I pause. This pause can be for 3 seconds or 3 days, however long it takes to become centered and peaceful again. By reading daily inspirational materials and meditating each day I have increased my conscious contact with God. God is no longer a feeling I seek—spiritual emotionalism misunderstood as the presence of God in my life—God is a fact, not a feeling. God is a living part of my consciousness and my life. My awareness of Divine Presence allows for days of usefulness and peace, which no longer depend on my emotions to guide my decisions or actions. Emotional balance is said to be the first fruit of meditation, and this was something that I not only wanted but seriously needed. Meditation, a time of quiet stillness, allows all to be still.

You should not miss out on meditation. My experience is that you will come to long for—your soul will need—these moments of time alone with Creator. I suggest committing to an appointed time each day, beginning before anything else. Some scoff at meditation but the scoffers usually have not tried persistently to meditate or asked for guidance from one who does. Maybe meditation for you will be one time a day or one time a week. Try to incorporate your time of quiet with God into your daily life—if you want the emotional balance that comes as a result of prayer and meditation.

Creating a sacred space for my daily prayer time has assisted in this time becoming integrated into my life. A personal altar with items that reflect the idea of your Higher Power, a picture, a rock, prayer books. The items will grow as you begin to create your sacred space. Do not limit your sacred space to indoors only as many places outside can become sacred to you as well. My sacred space supports an environment of calm and peace and life. Another thing that has helped me and I suggest to those who are "sensitive" to other feelings, illness, etc. is to include saying a prayer of protection. When I began to become conscious of my oneness with my Creator I began to realize my intuitive gifts and I had to learn the proper use of these gifts with guidance from a mature spiritual guide. I ask to be of service when and where I can. I do not need, nor does the world need me to carry the weight, illness or feelings of another. So I have written in the sidelines of my daily prayer book—so as to remember—to bathe in the light of the Spirit as a spiritual sunscreen for protection throughout the day. No need to take on those illnesses, injuries or emotions of another. As I have inventoried my life up—down—front—back I have come to see, admit and accept that I have—at some time—misused every God-given human and spiritual power ever given to me. The discipline of Step Eleven is the cement for the new direction my life has taken—this is my security as God is my source. Practicing this step—I can easily—after some time become centered as though the calm in the middle of the storm within my own mind and heart. And some moments allow for laughter to finds its way to the light of day as well.

Prayer

There seems to be a common format for universal prayers, suggested by the following outline, which may be used as a guide as some of you begin to learn to communicate with God through prayer. I have often heard that prayer is a time we talk to God and meditation is when we try to listen to God.

- Praise and thanksgiving—the fastest way to consciousness with God is to say "Thank You."

- Acknowledgment of the presence of a Higher Power/Creator/God—and this, my friend, is not you or me.

- Acknowledge God's Sovereignty/Dominion over all life—God is the One with all power.

- *Present needs and requests for others as well as yourself; avoid petitions that include yourself only. Be specific and honest as you share with God the needs and desire of your heart, adding "Thy will be done"—trusting in Creator's time and way.*

- Believe—Choose to trust that God is present and you are heard and cared for, in all things.

- Confess any wrongs committed and seek guidance for making amends.

- Forgive—Ask God to forgive you as well as anyone you may resent. Ask God to forgive others and/or yourself through you, with you as the channel for peace.

- Ask God for the Grace to do better, next time.

- Thank God for any job well done by you, and for the Grace and opportunity to be of service, and for your daily reprieve from the "problem" which separated you from conscious contact with God.

- Close with thanksgiving.

Now would be a good time to read sacred writings and then meditate for at least 5 minutes working your time up to an hour of meditation. This is to be an enjoyable and pleasurable time so that you look forward to returning to this communion each day. If you need to walk outside to commune with God, then have your time with God outside. Be creative, as this is your relationship with Creator, these are only guidelines to help you create a disciplined spiritual life.

One last thing about prayer: pray no matter what. Pray whether you believe or not. Pray no matter how you feel about God or yourself.

Pray, no matter what!

Meditation is as much a part of the Eleventh Step as prayer is. Do not miss this experience out of prejudice, fear or ignorance.

Meditation

Meditation cannot be done wrong. Just like anything else, this takes practice and effort to improve your meditation skills. It does get better with each attempt and effort.

Some tips that may help are:

If you feel bored, restless or your mind wanders that is okay. Use your breathing to bring your mind back to your quiet space. Focus on one word or two to repeat (a mantra, love, God, wisdom, breathe, peace, etc.). Prayer beads, a rosary, or holding a special object will also help you to focus your mind and relax at the same time as you go into a meditative state of consciousness.

If you fall asleep during your time of meditation it is because you need the sleep. Set a clock for your meditation time, so your mind does not worry. Make sure the alarm on the clock is set low enough to not be so intrusive that it is disturbing, yet, loud enough to gently wake you. Sleep is the time that the body repairs itself at a cellular level. So if you need it, sleep during this time.

If practicing at home with other people around, put a "Do NOT Disturb" sign on the door for 15 minutes. This works great after work to refresh the self for the rest of the day's commitments. Believe me a relaxed, rested you will improve the family's time with you and yours with them. And 15 minutes of *attempted* meditation is worth it.

- Use music, calm relaxing music.

- Burn incense (smell is the best way to communicate to your body that you are surrounded by a peaceful environment).

- Create a place of relaxation/restoration in your home, just for you!

- Journal after you meditate and write down your experience; review it after 30 days. You may journal through writing or drawing.

Enjoy your experience and your personal journey with meditation.

Chapter Eleven
STEP ELEVEN

Sought through prayer and meditation to improve our conscious contact with God as we understood Him/Her, praying only for knowledge of Divine will in our lives and the power to carry that out.

📖   ***Read*** "On Awakening…" every morning. (page 86 in *Alcoholics Anonymous*)

- Invite friends or family to join you in morning meditation, prayer at mealtime, or in the evening, invite another to share prayer with you at least once each day. This may be done over the phone if needed. Share a prayer with a child or reach out to anyone who is homebound, isolated from human Spiritual connection.

- Memorize and reflect on a few set prayers that support the principles you have just experienced in the previous ten steps. The Saint Francis prayer is but one that embodies these principles.

- Create a journal of prayers, your conversations with God about yourself and your life as well as your needs and include prayers that have been requested from others. This step suggests we not pray for ourselves only and you may find the best way you can assist another is to pray for them. We pray for others health happiness and prosperity, especially if we harbor ill feelings toward them.

- For the times when you are unable to pray, pray anyway. For the days you are unable to call upon your faith, call another and ask them to stand for you in prayer and faith, until you are free to believe again. Do not worry about the times you do not want to pray, to communicate with God, we all have difficulty at times in all relationships and this will pass, the day will come again where daily prayer is easy and enjoyable as it is part of your daily spiritual discipline. This will be your guide, a foundation no matter what storm comes upon you, prayer is a safe harbor. Memorizing sacred writings and prayers is also recommended for times when you are in need of focusing, connecting to God, to help direct your attention to what God would have you be or do.

PRINCIPLE *Discipline*

- Carve out time in your day where you secure silence to meditate, to refresh your spirit and mind. You deserve this each day—a time of loving communion with God. This may be a walk with God in the park or woods or time to be still in your sacred space that you have created.

- Take a day to experience creation, a day to be aware of the seasons, the weather, and any animals that you may see.

- Write the many ways you experience God's presence in your life today.

- Create a dream journal, if this is an interest, as God has historically used dream-time to communicate with us in many cultures. Pray before sleeping and write your dreams upon waking.

- Learn about your cultural spiritual beliefs and or customs, and honor them even if you choose not to participate.

- Meditate, beginning with 5 minutes at a time, each day. Be still, breathe and experience the God within you and surrounding you in the lives of others. Find books, tapes or instruction on meditation *this week*.

- Suggestions may be obtained from one's spiritual director or Church.

Read "When we retire…" every evening. (page 86 in *Alcoholics Anonymous*)

Daily prayer and meditation is a practice of spiritual discipline.

PRINCIPLE *Discipline*

"Blessed are the poor in spirit, for theirs is the kingdom of heaven.
Blessed are those who mourn, for they will be comforted.
Blessed are the meek, for they will inherit the earth.
Blessed are those who hunger for righteousness, for they will be filled.
Blessed are the merciful, for they will be shown mercy.
Blessed are the pure in heart, for they will see God.
Blessed are the peacemakers, for they will be called sons of God.
Blessed are those who are persecuted because of righteousness,
For theirs is the kingdom of heaven."
Matthew 5: 3-10

Chapter Twelve
Support for Step Twelve

SERVICE TO OTHERS and God is the idea of Step Twelve. Joy and hope is the message. Having received the healing grace of God, with a grateful heart I experience joy in living as I get up each day with new wonder at who I am and how I can add to the joy and well-being of another on life's journey. I may need to reflect and practice gratitude on those days I have difficulty seeing how my life has changed. Some people do not want an extraordinary life, but I do. I know that it is through continued surrender and trust that my life is anything but boring. I have had a Spiritual awakening, I am of service, and I trust God to meet my needs and manage my life. For my attitude to have been changed from one of self-centeredness to one of seeing how I can be of service is truly God restoring my soul. How can I add to the life of my family, friends? How can I be a blessing in each new day? That is the attitude that is developed—and for those still wondering, "What about me?" Such thinking is where I find misery—when I become absorbed with where and how I am getting or not getting what I want. Still, some days I need to visit that place until I become comfortable living in the realm of the spirit.

We carry into every area of our lives an attitude of service and gratitude. Service is an attitude and this is followed with action. That action is applying the principles in all areas of my life. To participate in my life and the lives of others sharing hope, love and joy.

Even if my time is limited each day. I pray and ask God how I can use my gifts to bless another. That is what you can do as well, ask to be used to bless others. Look in each day to see your awakening unfolding in your life. Reading the second step visions six months after completing this process will amaze you. It still amazes me what God can do when we put ourselves into His care.

The only thing I have seen that will break through and destroy the wall of fear is to be of service to God and others. Fear of people, fear of rejection, etc., will die as you uncover your purpose and your passion and live in the moment. Giving to others! That will walk you right past any fear of failure and feelings of inadequacy that you may have—and we all have some at times.

By this time it will no longer be about you—it will be about what you can give—how you can add to the world you live in. Feeling good about oneself is about being of service—no matter what age one may be. Healthy self-esteem is supported by this step and for some it is created with this step. Healthy and satisfying relationships are supported by carrying into the relationship the attitude of, "what can I do to demonstrate to this person—they are loved." If I have had prayer and meditation in each day, then I can assure you God will inspire, reveal or create an opportunity for me to demonstrate love. It may be as simple as a smile or for my husband—on days when I feel that internal nudging to act the service and love of Step Twelve—I make coffee for him as it is a big deal to have coffee when he wakes up in the morning. So when the nudging comes, I trust God knows more about what my husband needs and I hasten to demonstrate, in a way that he understands, that he matters and is important to me.

Look for the coincidences that begin to happen (in reality, you are just beginning to notice them). Ways that things happen "all of a sudden," "doors open" around your career or school. When we are working and walking hand in hand with the Spirit of the universe, trying to be of the best service, extraordinary things happen. Then those extraordinary things become ordinary and we reach higher—to live more fully in the realm of the Spirit. Living outside the realm becomes too uncomfortable. The joy of living is to be of service. No matter what age, marital status or sex, to be of service, using the gifts each of us has—not controlled by them or others— is truly to experience Heaven on Earth. No longer being filled with self-doubt but confidence you can look into each day seeing that you have a significant place and the opportunity to bless others' lives. You will find your needs and dreams fulfilled while you are looking the other way—serving God and others. Do you think our community, our families, our world can really afford to not have you give what you can of your time and experience of healing and hope? A kindness offered that will support the cycle of giving is what is asked here. And practicing the principles in all your affairs just becomes part of who you are!

I have to share with you that when I began to experience the word "bliss" and feel "wonder" as I rose from my bed each day with new expectation, I had a fear or more a question that needed an answer.

I called one of my spiritual advisors and told her I had a serious question to pose to her. She told me to go on. I asked her if I was about to die. I had heard or believed most of my life that people very close to "crossing" over, dying, become blissful, joyful beyond worldly description, very intuitive, etc. Was I about to die? Having found the happiness I had searched for and created the environment for God to restore me to my truest nature, I was concerned it was about to end.

She assured me this was not to be as this was what living was for. To live and experience happiness—joy and freedom. I did call her several times—as the bliss continued and my intuition grew and with each phone call she assured me—until that old idea was no longer with me. The kingdom of Heaven I had searched for was truly at hand, it is now, the last place I wanted to look, within my own being and within others as well, no matter how sick, God is within all of creation. It is good.

Reflect on the words of Rabindranath Tagore, winner of the Nobel Prize for Literature in 1913.

> ### *"I slept and I dreamed that life was all joy. I woke and saw that life was but service. I served and understood that service was joy."*

So walk with confidence, remembering we are not alone on this journey, although feelings of aloneness may come as you share bliss and joy in your daily lives. We walk together in peace, in joy and in hope for life that is grounded and perfected by love. Perfect and Divine love, the expression of a loving and powerful Creator encouraging us to enjoy and cherish this gift of life.

Today I have been restored to the wonder of a small child and the maturity of a responsible adult. Who could ask for more? May we meet in the cycle of giving, the cycle of loving, the cycle of life.

Chapter Twelve
STEP TWELVE

Having had a spiritual awakening as the result of these steps,
we tried to carry this message to others, and to practice
these principles in all our affairs.

📖 ***Read** pages 89—164 in Alcoholics Anonymous.*

✍ **Write a list of your gifts and talents to share with others in your home, community, workplace, twelve step group or church.**

✍ **Journal the many ways you experience God in your life today.**

Ideas to carry the message of hope to others:
- Reach out to the person you do NOT know in your support group or meeting.
- Write a letter or call someone who is suffering.
- Practice praying with those who are confined to their home.
- Pray for and seek volunteer opportunities in your church or community.
- Participate at home and work by practicing love and tolerance of others and an attitude of helpfulness.

Read your Step Two, Step Three and Step Four vision statements.

Practice Steps Ten, Eleven and Twelve daily to support your spiritual awakening.

It may be uncomfortable for you as well as others as you adjust to being the more authentic you! Balance will come with practice. Enjoy.

Sponsor/support/encourage others by offering guidance in working the steps—that they too may find a God who can solve their problems and who will bring about the necessary physic change.

Maintain your relationship with your Spiritual Director—someone who can guide you in continued spiritual growth and accountability. This will help you to avoid the pitfall of spiritual arrogance.

PRINCIPLE *Service*

"For the Lord is good and his love endures forever;
his faithfulness continues through all generations."
Psalm 100: 5

Chapter Thirteen
Where From Here?

BY THIS TIME, you may have found six to nine months have gone by and maybe even a year. You may have feelings of not wanting this process to end if you have experienced this within a group setting. You will be going to scheduled meetings each week or each month to share and give support to others who have watched you change. Some of you may be aware of major life decisions and action taken while using this workbook; others might not be so aware right now of the changes and should ask others for affirmation. Over the course of your transformation, relations with family and friends may have settled; some of these people may have left. If they have left then it is because they were not there for your support to begin with.

Healthy love supports personal growth—it does not take hostages. I know when my loved ones grow and change, as uncomfortable as it may be for me at the moment, they will become more true to themselves and therefore we will have a more true and authentic relationship. Be kind to your family and friends as they adjust to the more accurate reflection of your true nature that is manifesting. It may take them time to be assured they have a place in your restored life.

For me, change came slowly at first. The first time I used these tools, my brain had difficulty coming out of the fog of denial. I went through this process again within a year and found it much easier. This time I was asked to guide some women through a similar process and found that the changes I experienced were more profound, although it appeared that my life was falling apart, literally. I now realize that it was being dismantled in order to be restored—put back together in a more loving and useful way. When I made a commitment to lead this group of women, the early development for this workbook became my anchor for the next nine months. This group of twelve women fulfilled a commitment to each other to complete a step study process during that time. And during that same nine months I experienced the death of one of my dearest friends, my husband became very ill and disabled, my employer did not pay me money I had earned—so that I was jobless when I had to undergo emergency surgery. Yet during that time, too, an inaccurate diagnosis of a mental disorder, for which I had been treated over a period of twelve years, was finally disproven and withdrawn. My life was transformed, and as I continued creating this workbook over the next few years and working these steps my life became something I wanted; I began to live my dreams. Today my Second Step restoration and spiritual awakening is still unfolding—and I am letting it. I have done my part. It is now time for me to enjoy the unfolding of God's plan.

You may find yourself in a new career, driving a new car, changing your residence, entertaining a marriage proposal, making new decisions regarding your education. You may have lost your appetite for certain foods—the very foods you once thought you could not live without. You may have put out that last cigarette. That is what the outside may look like, but what about the inside—your heart—your mind—your thinking? According to A.A. literature, our problem is centered in the mind. That is precisely why a *physic change* is needed.

You may be glad to awaken each day confident as you are relying on Spirit to walk with you and guide you each day. You may find many opportunities to bless someone. Maybe a stranger; maybe your family or friends or support group or church, synagogue or compatriots. Your emotions are balanced as a result of practicing the discipline of daily self-examination, prayer and meditation. Joy and bliss may now be your partner, replacing fear and pain.

You may now have a relationship with God that is more precious than you could have imagined and evolved new ways to share love everyday. You may now want to review your Step Two vision statements. If you keep on, you will find that the person you were created to be is in part a loving expression of Divine Creator. You are blessed and blessing the world with unique qualities, gifts and talents that make this world a better place. You are now able to receive and give—graciously and humbly.

Where you go from here is really up to you. Teach your children by example if you are blessed with children. Teach your parents by example if you are blessed with living parents. Let others see who you are by how you live, practicing "principles over personalities."

Practice the principles each day to the best of your ability and begin this process all over again when the time is right—you will know when it is time. Encourage others in the use of this workbook so they too may know a simple means of how to remember who they are created to be—as human spiritual beings.

The following chapters give guidelines and suggestions for creating and facilitating a group for those who, like you, desire restoration and seek spiritual growth. You cannot go about this in a wrong way as long as you are honest and respectful of others.

At first you may find living in the "realm of the Spirit" on a daily basis to be unfamiliar and awkward. You may even retrieve some of those old trusted character defects, when you become afraid. That is okay, we all do this from time to time. That is why we *practice* the principles. For me it is like learning to walk. We applaud the efforts of a small child to grow and learn, we even applaud every step. Even when children fall down and scrape their knees, we treat them with kindness and are in wonder at the determination they have to keep going until they take each step with confidence. Yet when we fall, we criticize ourselves. Applaud your efforts and know it will become more comfortable and easier to live this life filled with wonder, this life of love and unselfishness, a life with principles. With gentle kindness honor the creation that you are. With the practice of honest self-appraisal in Step Ten and daily practice of time and communion with God each day, I assure you that the principles you have put into practice will soon become part of your nature, the nature that is truly your most authentic self.

"*37 Jesus replied: 'Love the Lord your God with all your heart and with all your soul and with all your mind.' 38 This is the first and greatest commandment. 39 And the second is like it: 'Love your neighbor as yourself.'"*
Matthew 22: 37-39

Chapter Fourteen
Guide for Step Studies
Facilitator's Guide

*Information, Agenda and Facilitator's Guide for the
Introduction to a Step Study Meeting using this Workbook.*

- Welcome
- Introduce yourself and ask others to introduce themselves.
- Share your hopes, for yourself by working the steps with this group.
- Review the Facilitator's Guide—Initial Meeting pages.
- Share brief quotes from the book *Alcoholics Anonymous,* and your personal experience with the twelve steps that offers promise, choosing examples that address spiritual conditions. *Set* expectations, set forth what is to be "hoped for," and share what you have seen with those you know who have completed this process.

This workbook is an adaptation of the twelve steps from A.A. and is a guide using various tools that have been effective in assisting numerous others in using an adaptation of the twelve steps to bring about the desired and necessary changes and healing in one's life. Many of the questions asked in this guide are from the book, *Alcoholics Anonymous,* commonly referred to as the "Big Book."

An A.A. or twelve step group is not a place for this type of step study, as this is a closed meeting/group after the first meeting. In accordance with A.A.'s Traditions, an A.A. meeting must be open at any time to anyone desiring to stay sober, unless arrangements have been made (paying rent to the group for this meeting) that do not violate the group's traditions or bylaws. A study of this workbook is not a meeting of Alcoholics Anonymous, and is not intended to take the place of a twelve step meeting or professional help. Rather it is intended as a gathering of individuals who desire to work each of the twelve steps in depth, with a group, in order to experience healing and personal spiritual growth.

After the first meeting of those who have committed to the process, the group should not be open to others. This will allow the group to move forward, building intimacy and avoiding discrimination and preferential treatment. Adhering to agreed boundaries will help participants to practice the discipline of honoring commitments to the group, and this in turn will build trust and feelings of safety as sharing begins. If arrangements are made with a twelve step group or club to use space for those engaged in this step study and an agreed-upon monetary payment for this space as a way of paying 'rent'—then there may be no conflict with any group's traditions. Check with the bylaws of your twelve step group first if you plan on holding your closed study group on a twelve step group's premises. A committed support person is essential through this process.

Chapter Fourteen

Facilitator's Guide—Initial Meeting
Information for Step Study Meeting

Have this meeting at least four weeks prior to starting a step study so that each person has adequate time to decide about committing and to review the material. When people are clear about the level of commitment and expectation, most are able to follow through and complete the study.

Step Study will be held at _____ (location) _____ (time).
Meetings are typically 90 minutes in length. Allow time to arrive early or stay late for fellowship, as meetings begin and end on time.

It is strongly suggested that the group meet for study at the same place each week. This will eliminate confusion and allow ease in locating the meeting.

Guidelines: These are to support—rebuild/build a sense of safety, security, trust and to practice discipline, honor and respect.

One facilitator is needed for this process, but members may share in the leading of opening and closing the meeting. You may need co-facilitators if the group is more than the ideal size of 10-12 people. If co-facilitators are needed, the meetings begin and end together—with members breaking-out into small groups in between. Remember, there is one facilitator for guiding the entire group.

- Hand out *Remembering Who We Are: A Workbook* for review.

- Review the use of Mind Mapping.

- Ask potential step study members to pray and decide if they will commit to the step study.

- Please call and give your commitment, directly to the facilitator, one week prior to the beginning date of the step study.

- After the first step study meeting, the group is closed to additional attendees.

- For those participating in this step study you will need to read the Facilitator's Guide, pages 169-177 <u>before</u> the first meeting.

- At the first meeting, those who commit to this process should be prepared to disclose the "ONE THING" they are powerless over, for Step One. Examples of the "ONE THING" that is currently causing unmanageability in your life could be: alcohol, drugs, food, sex, gambling, work, death, illness, children/parents/people, rage, stealing, etc. It is suggested that only one topic be picked and written under "powerless." The First Step does not say we are powerless over the alcoholic, it says we are "powerless over alcohol," no matter who is using it. So I am powerless over alcohol, work, drugs, food, rage, sex, etc., even if someone else abuses alcohol, work, drug use, food, etc., this can create unmanageability in my life.

- What is the "ONE THING" that is standing in the way of my happiness and peace of mind and creating unmanageability in my life? You may not put yourself or your name as this item.

- At the first meeting, after you share what you are powerless over, share what your hope is for yourself or your intention as a participant of this step study.

- The facilitator will share his/her entire First Step at the first meeting with the group. Subsequently his/her work at the beginning of each step will be shared, in order to provide leadership by example.

- No one will share their Fifth Step with the group.

- Please bring your workbook, *Alcoholics Anonymous*, and personal notebook to each meeting.

- Discuss creating a sacred space—as discussed on page 174.

- This group will decide at the first meeting any dates they will not meet, i.e. holidays, etc.

- It is very important to begin and end each meeting at the agreed upon time.

You cannot do the steps wrong.

Each person will have a different experience.

Chapter Fourteen

Group Conscience Decisions
to be made at the First Meeting

First Meeting

- Will smudging or lighting a candle be used to assist in creating and reminding each member of the Sacred Space created during each meeting? The group may suggest other ways to support creating a Sacred Space. The facilitator is to be prepared to lead in the creation of a sacred space.

- Are there any holidays or dates when the group will not meet, i.e. meet every Sunday, except the last Sunday of each month.

- Make a phone and email list for communication once the step study has begun.

- Email is to be used solely for step study communication unless prior permission is given.

Guidelines

Guidelines are to create and support a safe and honored space for all participants. They should exemplify the practice of principles before personalities.

- Unless professionally facilitated, these should be same-sex meetings.
- After the beginning of step study, these are closed meetings.
- *Confidentiality* is respected at these meetings! What is said MUST stay in the meeting. No gossip or criticism of one another or another's situation in or outside of the meeting. Share *your* experience with this process, not another's.
- Follow through with your commitment to the work and attend each meeting. Be there for the group not just for yourself!
- **Arrive and begin the meeting at the agreed upon time and close on time. This allows practice of positive discipline and demonstrates respect for other's precious time. Each person will need to arrive before the opening to allow for time needed to get settled into the group meeting.**
- Kleenex should be available in the center of the room so that anyone can ask for it or easily get it for themselves. Offering Kleenex to another, unasked, can often stop feelings from being expressed.
- You will need the book *Alcoholics Anonymous* as a reference as you work in this workbook. This may be purchased at any bookstore or from your local Alcoholics Anonymous group. And each person will need this workbook prior to the beginning of the study. The facilitator or other designated person may order the workbooks for those in the study.

Housekeeping Items and Attendance Guidelines

- No tobacco use or eating during meeting.
- Meeting begins at __o'clock sharp and ends promptly at __o'clock.
- If you are going to miss a meeting please call the facilitator prior to the start of the meeting.
- Place of meeting will be open for fellowship 30 minutes before and 30 minutes after step study.
- Coffee will be available (bring water or soda if you desire) but please avoid getting up and down during the meeting as this disrupts the sharing of feelings and feelings of intimacy are easily broken when members are moving around.
- Group decides the day to begin and goal date to end the study group. Set the date for desired completion.
- Agree upon holidays when the group will not be meeting. *The facilitator will bring calendar to first official meeting and a phone list for members.*
- The phone list or email list is for members of the group only unless permission for other use is given by individual members.
- Assist in the cleanup after each meeting.

Step study will be held at _____ (location) _____ (date/time).
It is strongly suggested that the study meet at the same place and at the same time each week. Doing so will eliminate possible confusion as to where and when to meet.

The step study will be sharing their First, Second and Third Steps with the group.
The group will say the Third Step prayer together. *The Fourth Step will not be shared within the group meeting.* Experiences with writing the Fourth Step and Fifth Step may be shared. Each person will share Sixth Step mind-mapping work with the group and the Seventh Step mind map and prayer is offered together as a group. The Step Eight through Step Twelve experiences are shared while following the order of the workbook.

Meeting Structure Format

The same facilitator will lead each meeting. Other members of the study may be invited to lead the opening or the closing prayer. With every meeting it must be kept in mind that the facilitator's guidance is to be trusted. Step study is an individual experience and members of the group must refrain from 'therapy type' feedback, criticism, gossip and confrontation offering other members encouragement with brief words of respect and honor. There is no place for judgment within this process and all participants should remember that the God of all Creation, along with principles of love and honesty, are to be the ultimate guide in situations that may arise. Individual and private sharing of experience, strength and hope, as well as referrals to professionals, constitute a loving form of support for those who experience difficulties during this process that require outside assistance. Remember that no one personally dominates or controls the meetings. The facilitator lovingly guides the meeting, allowing each person ample time for sharing; participants help by trying not to exceed their fair share of the time available for the meeting.

Create a Sacred Space!

The intention is to create a sacred space to hold your meetings for sharing of trust and honesty and to create an atmosphere of safety, respect and confidentiality.

Open with Suggested Reading

Open with a common and agreed upon prayer; samples can be found at the back of this workbook. In order to connect and get centered with purpose and presence, light a candle and smudge if this is desired and agreed upon by the group and then breathe rhythmically for a few minutes. Observe several minutes of silence. Each individual should focus on why he or she is present and silently invite the Spirit of God to be present throughout the meeting. Try focusing on the group collectively as well as individually. Remembering in silent prayer those who are absent.

What is Smudging?

This is a Native American practice and you may decline if you choose. Smudging is always an option for each person and is merely a suggestion as given here. Smudging is a way to cleanse the environment or person from stress, negativity, worry, fatigue, etc., and the quiet process allows for the centering of each person's spirit and body in the presence of Divine Creator. Sage is typically the plant that is used (cedar or sweet grass is also used at times).

To smudge simply place a small amount of Sage in an abalone shell, light it and give it a few seconds to burn and give off smoke. The facilitator then holds the shell in front of one person at a time. The smoke is then embraced and brushed with the hands over heart, mind, hands, etc., while each person is breathing quietly and praying, asking God to be present and to create a Sacred Space. The shell is passed around until everyone who desires has been smudged. While others are smudging the group remains silent and supports the person smudging with silent prayer or mindfulness. This only takes a few minutes and is a wonderful way to leave the outside world to become totally present. You may purchase sage from various stores that sell organic foods or Native American products.

The Meeting Outline

1. Create a sacred space.

2. Review agenda for meeting.

   - What step for this week?
   - Who is sharing their step work, sign up for sharing of Step One and Two.
   - Share step work in order of signup.
   - If time allows go around the room so that each person may share where they are with the step they are on! Try to stay focused on where you are with this process in your life today. What is going on in your step work/how is it showing up in your life…what are you experiencing?
   - At the end the facilitator will review next week's work and answer questions.

3. Each person will share his/her First Step mind mapping work, with NO EXPLANATIONS and NO questioning from members listening. Just read and allow the Light of the Spirit to support you, as your courage is a grace bestowed by honesty.

   - After you finish reading your step work, pause and breathe and make *eye contact* with each person present. Next, pause to hear brief words of support, affirmations and encouragement, if you would like the other group members to offer their support. Sample words might be: "You are so courageous and honest" or "I really relate—my Step One is similar to yours, thanks for taking the risk and trusting."
   - Remember that another's reality or situation is not to be judged. The point is to share what the powerlessness and unmanageability in your life is like for you at your current stage of life. When ready, the facilitator will move on to the next person committed to read his/her step work. Repeat.
   - Repeat this process with Step Two, reading only the vision statements for each area of restoration. With the reading of the Step Two vision statements the group may feel like bursting into applause! That is also a great show of support and as with some of the next steps the shared writings and experience will elicit applause, laughter, tears, and feelings of joy.

If individuals need to create an index card to hold as they read their work with a reminder to focus on reading the mind maps words, this may help those accustomed to explaining.

NO EXPLANATION IS NEEDED. It is what it is—read your written work!

The facilitator reminds each person reading to breathe or to slow down as they read their mind maps and to remember that no explanation is needed. However, if explanations are given, love and kindness should determine the response, as each of us responds differently to fear and feeling vulnerable. It is easy to talk fast, avoid eye contact or make jokes to avoid feelings of vulnerability and intimacy.

If no one is sharing step work, then any time left for sharing may be focused upon the step each person is currently experiencing or working on.

4. Review for next meeting, those who will be sharing their step work. Review "how to" for the next chapter of step work for those who have shared and are ready to move to the next chapter. If anyone is unclear about "how to" with some of the step work, call the facilitator between meetings for support or guidance.

5. Remind participants to reach out to each other in the weeks to come—make phone calls daily giving or receiving support and encouragement.

6. Read the closing.

7. Gather in circle and say the chosen prayer for that meeting.

Sample Prayers and Procedures

Opening

We gather in the Spirit of Trust and Confidentiality to learn and practice the principles from the twelve steps of Alcoholics Anonymous. We are reminded to speak and act from our hearts, hearts that are open, loving, and respectful of others' rights. We DO NOT offer opinions or critiques about others' situations and we agree that what is said here, stays here.

This process was designed to restore us, that we may participate more completely in our family and community life and assume our role as children of God.

Opening Prayer

Choose a common prayer, such as part of the Serenity Prayer or Our Father, a song or other words or music selected by the facilitator.

Centering and Creating of Sacred Space

There are a variety of ways to create a sacred space - following are examples but not limitations to use in creating a sacred space for your group. Use of breathing, smudging, lighting a candle, listening to music or other inspired ways, will help the group to center and set the intention for a protected and sacred space, each member inviting the Spirit of God to be present.

Closing

In closing, we honor the vulnerability that has enabled us to share so honestly. We respectfully ask Creator's Spirit to work within our group conscience to protect our confidentiality. In the week to come, we ask for guidance for our thoughts, words and actions that we may be led deeper into our hearts, hearts that are open and loving. We offer no gossip or criticism of each other, but instead ask that the love and peace at this gathering might grow in us one day at a time.

Closing Prayer

Together pray a common prayer, song or a variety of prayers or use the suggestion below.

For a varied closing prayer have each person within the group bring a prayer or a song of prayerful intent that reflects his or her culture, heritage, or faith. Share a copy with each member of the group for use during the closing prayer.

ABOUT THE AUTHOR

"Supporting, guiding and teaching another in a transitional healing process is a privilege and honor. To be invited into the sacred space of another for healing, from birth through death, is an invitation to celebrate the preciousness and wonder of each creation and of the Creator."

Carol Ann Preston has over 25 years of experience developing and teaching award-winning programs for adolescents and adults. These programs embrace the many ways that each of us grows and is renewed, individually and collectively addressing issues such as grief and dying, addictions, parenting, child abuse, domestic violence, family systems, and guided meditation, as well as the use and practice of twelve step spirituality.

Carol began dealing with death at age 8 when she witnessed her grandfather's death. It was during the late '70s that she began to work as a volunteer in her community to gain support for abused children. She later became a doula, a professional coach for pregnant women and women in labor. In dealing with a stillborn child, and because of numerous loved ones who died within a relatively short time, Carol recognized her gift as a *midwife to the soul*, a gift handed down from generations of women before her. Over the past 15 years she has supported numerous families, including her own friends and family, in the process of dying and grieving, each time learning more about the gift of love and the journey of death and grief.

Carol has continued in her volunteerism for over 25 years, encouraging her children to do the same within their communities. She was invited to Sydney, Australia, during the Olympics/Paralympics in 2000, being selected as a volunteer massage therapist by the medical director with the IOC on the basis of her experience with the disabled and advanced training in medical and sport massage. Carol is licensed as a massage therapist in Texas. She is also a Reiki teacher, using this healing art to assist those who desire healing by this means.

Carol has loved writing since her early teens, and writes both fiction and nonfiction. Within each work she incorporates a spiritual foundation of character and principle.

Over the past 20 years Carol has taught religious education to children and teens at her church, and has developed and presented programs and retreats on twelve step spirituality to various groups, including a local Jesuit Retreat Center, and she has facilitated numerous groups of men and women using the twelve step guide she has written. She recently realized a lifelong dream of being an Extraordinary Eucharist Minister and currently works as a hospital chaplain in Texas. Carol is married, with two grown children, and two grandchildren. Her hobbies include photography and rose gardening.

You may request workshops, retreats or presentations by contacting Carol at www.roomforhealing.com. You may also receive support and encouragement online at www.recoverycrossroads.com in the forum section under "Room for Healing". Read Carol's weekly column online at www.recoverylife.com, "Weekly journeys into the Realm of the Spirit". Carol is a regular guest on KHLT Broadcasting's Take 12 Recovery Radio Show with Monty Meyer (The Monty'man). The Take 12 show broadcast 24 hours a day 7 days a week. To tune in visit: www.take12radio.com.

Lightning Source UK Ltd.
Milton Keynes UK
UKOW02f0703101213

222709UK00005B/205/A